THE
Heinemann
English
PROGRAMME

3

John Seely   David Kitchen

With Special Project by

Christopher Stubbs

Heinemann

Heinemann Educational Publishers
Halley Court, Jordan Hill, Oxford OX2 8EJ
A Division of Reed Educational & Professional Publishing Ltd

**OXFORD MELBOURNE AUCKLAND
JOHANNESBURG BLANTYRE GABORONE
IBADAN PORTSMOUTH (NH) USA CHICAGO**

First published 1995

2004 2003 2002 2001 2000
21 20 19 18 17 16 15

British Library Cataloguing in Publication data
for this title available from the British Library.

ISBN 0 435 10356 3

Designed and produced by Gecko Limited, Bicester, Oxon

Printed in Spain by Mateu Cromo

Acknowledgements

The authors would like to thank the following people for their help with
this book:

- Instructors and administrative staff at *PGL Young Adventures*,
  Ross-on-Wye
- Margaret and Charlotte Garnett
- The Headteacher, teachers and pupils at St Mary's School,
  Fownhope

We would like to thank the following for permission to reproduce
copyright material:

BBC Radio 4 for an extract from the transcript of 'In Touch' (14 February
1995); Kyle Cathie Ltd for 'Cheers whistles it's a driving test' from *If the
Sun Doesn't Kill You the Washing Machine Will* by Peter Wood; Daily
Express for 'Parents bet on exam children' by Jack Lee; Faber and Faber
for an extract from *Invisible Friends* by Alan Ayckbourn; Blake
Friedmann, Literary, TV & Film Agency, for 'Song of the Banana Man' by
Evan Jones; Victor Gollancz for cover of *Ringworld* by Larry Niven and
for *Aztec Century* by Christopher Evans; Hilary Gray and *Catch* magazine
for article on Brookside character; Gwen Grice for an extract from *The
Oak and the Ash* by Frederick Grice published by Oxford University
Press; HarperCollins Publishers Ltd for an extract from *Beyond Lands of
Never* by M. Jakubowski and for 'Conversation Piece' from *Salford Road*
by Gareth Owen; David Higham Associates for an extract from *The Day
of the Triffids* by John Wyndham published by Penguin Books; The
Independent for 'Pure genius in the making of a can' by Steve Connor (19
September 1994); Philip Larkin for 'Take one Home for the Kiddies' by
Philip Larkin; Larousse PLC for an extract from *Pocket Planet Earth* by
Martyn Bramwell published by Kingfisher, copyright © Grisewood &
Dempsey Ltd 1991; Little Brown for the cover of *Alien* by Alan Dean
Foster reproduced by courtesy of Warner Books copyright Twentieth
Century Fox, and for the cover of *Black Unicorn* reproduced by courtesy
of Orbit Books. Cover illustration by Dave Pether; *More* magazine for
articles on Jon Bon Jovi and Pamela Anderson; Orchard Books for 'Sister
in a Whale' from *Taking my Pen for a Walk* by Julie O'Callaghan. First
published in the UK by Orchard Books, a division of The Watts Publishing
Group, 96 Leonard St, London EC2A 4RH; Oxford University Press for an
extract from the Oxford English Dictionary Second Edition on CD; Brian
Patten for 'The River's Story' by Brian Patten; Penguin Books for an
extract from *Through Brown Eyes* by Prafulla Mohanti; Peters Fraser &
Dunlop Group for 'On and On' from *Lucky* by Roger McGough; Radio
Times for an extract from the *Clive Doig Radio Times Puzzle Book*;
Reed Consumer Books for an extract from *The Monster Garden* by
Vivien Alcock published by Methuen Children's Books; Sight Savers
International for Blinking Hell advertisement; Transworld Publishers Ltd
for the cover of *Into the Labyrinth* by Weis and Hickman and the cover
of *Conquerors' Pride* by Zahn and for an extract from *Wings* by Terry
and Lynn Pratchett; Barrie Wade for 'Coming Late' by Barry Wade from
Barley Barley published by Oxford University Press.

Every effort has been made to contact copyright holders. We would be
glad to rectify any omissions at the next reprint if notice is given to the
publisher.

We would like to thank the following for permission to reproduce the
photos on the pages noted:

Cecil Beaton/Camera Press: p22 (Monroe); Berriedale-Johnson/Panos
Pictures: p129; Camera Press: pp22 (Mandela, Kahn) 24 (Prince); J. Allan
Cash: pp7 (mountaineers and rafting), 26 (beach house and Manhattan),
170; Donald Cooper: p139; Ben Costor/Camera Press: pp22 (Campbell),
24 (Moss); Nancy Durrell-McKenna/Panos Pictures: p130; Erma/Camera
Press: p25 (Madonna); Mary Evans Picture Library: p170; Marc French/
Panos Pictures: pp124, 126; Gail Goodyer/Hutchinson: p26 (house
interior); Sally and Richard Greenhill: p7 (playground); Michael
Johannsson/Repfoto: p29; Kudos/Rex Features: p27; Lapance/Rex
Features: p7 (trucks in rally); Michael Linssen/Redferns: p22 (Jackson);
Peter Loughran/Reed International Books: p42; Richard Open/Camera
Press: p22 (Brand, Collins); David Poole/Robert Harding Picture Library:
p62; John Seely: pp8, 9, 10, 11, 12, 13, 14, 59, 97, 122, 154, 155, 156;
Sean Sprague/Panos Pictures: p131; Storm Stanley/Robert Harding
Picture Library: p62; Mark Steward/Camera Press: p22 (Thatcher);
Today/Rex Features: p25 (Akabussi); Sian Trenbath/Camera Press: p22
(Giggs); Vienna Report/Camera Press: p22 (Agassi); Tom Wargacki/
Camera Press: p28; Philip Wolmuth/Panos Pictures: p125.

Introduction

The Heinemann English Programme Book 3 offers a range of lively, enjoyable materials to help you develop your abilities in reading, writing, and speaking and listening.

Each unit contains a rich mix of fiction (stories, poems, playscripts), non-fiction (autobiography, information writing, newspapers, magazine articles) and activities based on a theme.

In each unit you will also find activities to develop your knowledge of and skills in **Language Study**. You will learn best about spelling, grammar and punctuation when these things are related to your own reading, writing, and speaking and listening. That is why the language activities in this book are all part of thematic units.

The **Special Projects** offer opportunities to work in groups, solve problems together and develop your skills in reading and writing in a variety of forms.

The Heinemann English Programme will help you to assess your own work so you can see how you are progressing in English. The grids at the beginning of each unit explain what you do and why you do it. In the Teacher's File which accompanies this book you will find student self-assessment sheets with guidance on assessing your work.

The Teacher's File also contains details of curriculum coverage for each unit, information about Language Study, a guide to the differentiation strategy in *The Heinemann English Programme*, photocopiable support and extension sheets, drama activities and assessment guidance.

We hope you find all *The Heinemann English Programme* has to offer interesting, useful and, above all, enjoyable.

Key to symbols in this book

TF	There is an extension or support worksheet for this activity available in the Teacher's File.

EXT	This is an extension piece suitable for more able students.

Contents

Action pack

Page	Title	What you do	Why you do it
7	**Action pack**	Look at the pictures and think and talk about different types of adventure.	To start you thinking about the themes of the unit.
8–14	**Adventure holidays**	Read the words of two interviews about adventure holidays and look at photographs of them. Answer questions on the text.	To focus on one aspect of adventure and learn in more detail about adventure holidays. To prepare for the next set of activities.
15	**'Adventure and fun in a framework of safety'**	Use the material you have been reading to write in the form of a magazine or a leaflet.	To help you plan, research, and complete a piece of work effectively. To develop your ability to write for a particular audience and purpose.
16	**Explaining abseiling**	Read the information in the interview on abseiling more closely and study the pictures. Work out exactly what the text means and write a clear explanation. Use a partner to help with your final version.	To improve your reading and writing skills, with particular emphasis on explaining. To use drafting.
17	**Speech and writing**	Compare speech and writing, looking for the changes that take place when we turn a piece of speech into a written text.	To improve your understanding of how language works. To improve your writing skills.
18–20	**Castaway**	Read a text written in the eighteenth century carefully and answer the questions. Imagine that Selkirk had lived today, and write an account of his adventures as it might be presented in modern media.	To improve your reading skills. To learn how to present information for different purposes and audiences.
21	**Words Wordpower**	Group words with similar meanings according to how they are used. Study words that appear in the unit.	To develop your vocabulary and to improve your spelling.

· ACTION PACK ·

Discuss: what is an adventure?

1 What does the word *adventure* mean to you?
2 Do any of these pictures suggest adventure to you?
3 If so, which one(s) and why?
4 What would be your ideal adventure?

Adventure holidays

One kind of adventure is offered by companies which provide adventure holidays. On the next few pages we look at some of the things that happen on an adventure holiday.

At PGL Adventure, children and young people from all over Britain are introduced to many different outdoor activities. During their holiday they are divided into groups. Each group is the responsibility of a **Group Leader**, or 'Groupie'. Each of the different activities is organised by one or more **Activity Instructors**.

We interviewed a Groupie and an Activity Instructor, to find out what they do on an adventure holiday.

What to do

1 Read the text on pages 9–14 and look at the pictures.
2 On pages 9, 11 and 13 there are questions to help focus your reading. Make sure that you can answer these before moving on to the next page.
3 When you have finished reading page 14, look at page 15 to find out what to do next.

Note: We have quoted their words exactly. Where you see words in square brackets – [ ] – these have been added by us to make the text easier to understand.

Meet the Groupie

A Groupie – is often the first contact they [the children] have when they come to a PGL centre.

[When they arrive] we're the ones that are there to put them in their groups, give them a tour round the centre, show them where they can go; what they can use; where all the facilities are. Once they feel happy in their room and they've seen where they're going to stay, you get the ball rolling: get some activities going.

A normal day would start with Wake Up which is 7–7.15 in the morning. We're the ones that run round and tell them to wake up [and] make sure everyone is OK. We make sure they go for a wash, give them a shower, [and] make sure they're going to do their teeth. Then [we] get them through breakfast. There's often one or two who don't feel like eating the first morning. That's quite important [to] sit with them during their breakfast, get them ready for their activities.

We're not there to instruct, we're there to be with them all the time, so we join them on all the activities but we're not instructing, we're there to relate to. You might take them abseiling for the morning [so you] make sure they're wearing all the right clothes. It sounds a bit funny but you make sure they're all warm. If they're going sailing [you] make sure they've got a spare set of clothes for when they might get wet [and] stay with them all through the day.

Questions

1 What do the Groupies do when new guests arrive?
2 What do the Groupies do each morning?
3 How would you sum up the work of a Groupie?

The Activity Instructor

We operate a range of activities from abseiling right the way through to slightly more fun aspects such as the assault course.

40   You have two types of canoeing: kayak, which is the closed boat, and Canadian or open kayak canoeing which are the larger open canoes. The instructor starts with a land-based demonstration on the kayak and also the paddle: how to hold the paddle and the correct stroke done on land. Once the instructor's happy then they will let them go on to the

50   water. There will be a safety boat on

the water and there will be an instructor already on the water in a kayak, so if somebody capsizes the instructor will be able to go over and help that person either out of their kayak or turn the kayak back over and empty the water out of it.

Motor sports: we have the quad bikes. They're four wheel with large tyres. A very simple course would just be a large circle or figure of 8 and you'll have a series of instructors positioned at key points around the course and maybe two quad bikes going around the course at suitable intervals apart from each other. It is basically fun; the kids tend to enjoy that. It's probably one of their more favoured activities.

60

Questions

4 How many different activities are mentioned on these two pages?

5 What evidence is there that PGL are safety-conscious?

6 What extra information do you get from the pictures that is not in the text?

The abseil tower

***Groupie*:**

70   A lot of teachers come away and – it's an eye-opener – they see some of the quietest children in the class suddenly become very very loud, very happy – you know – really really enjoying themselves. Some of the loudest people in the class suddenly, perhaps, go to pieces at the sight of an abseil tower.

***Instructor*:**

        You might have a group of five eleven-year-olds, and you'll nearly always have a natural leader within that group: someone who is perhaps more articulate, more confident, more outgoing. If you
80   get those five children on an abseil tower you'll find that it is not necessarily their elected leader [who] is the person who is the most confident. For an eleven-year-old abseiling down a forty-foot tower – no matter how safe we know it is – there is still an element of fear.

        Abseiling is done at most centres from a purpose-built tower. They're normally $37\frac{1}{2}$ feet tall. There [are] two instructors at the top;
90   the group leader and a third instructor at the bottom organising the groups waiting to go up on the tower.

        The lead instructor [goes] through the various pieces of equipment: what they are used for and the names of that equipment. They show them how to put the equipment on.

        When the instructor has donned the equipment they then go up to the top of the tower. You have two ropes: the abseiler abseils down the one rope
100   and is also attached to a second rope which is controlled at all times by an instructor. Therefore there is absolutely no way that the guests can fall.

The instructor abseils down from the tower to show the techniques: the wrong ways to abseil and the right ways to abseil – the distance apart the feet need to be, the angle at which you need to lean over, and various other things

110 The instructor picks who they think are the more competent people to start with so that their peers can see: 'Well, if they can do it I can do it.' Then the middle section of the group will be those people who are slightly less confident because again you don't want to leave them until the end, because it is longer for them to stew. And you finish the group again with more confident people.

Groupie:

120 I remember sitting at the bottom of abseil towers and people [say], 'I can't do that! I can't do that!' Then they go and have a go and they thoroughly enjoy it and they go back again. So they've … overcome … a fear of heights.

Questions

7 What is abseiling?
8 What do Jo and Steve think it can tell us about people?
9 How do the instructors make sure it is safe?

One big adventure

Groupie:

No two days are the same, none at all. You might just be eating your dinner and somebody is shouting they've lost their purse, they've lost
130 their Mars bar – and of course it means an awful lot losing their Mars bar to a seven-year-old.

There's always the weather. Maybe you go out there and one minute it is really really nice and the next it is really pouring and you realise half your group haven't got a waterproof with them. It's a long long day … a lot of stamina needed
140 … a lot of always smiling …

You're working with children all

the time – you either love being with a group of children or you don't. On a Monday you get a coach in; there's fifty children looking really like: 'Who are these people running round, all got nicknames, all looking silly?' And then by the end of the week they're crying their eyes out because [they] don't want
150 to go home, and you get letters back. That's really really rewarding when you get a load of letters: 'Dear DJ, Thank you … this that and the other …' – tell you all what they've done at school once they got back. It's just so nice. They come back year after year some of them. I just love it.

The job of a Groupie is a fun job for people that don't want to grow up. It's
160 one big adventure – for the staff as well: having a go at things you'd never dream of doing.

'Adventure and fun in a framework of safety'

Choose one of the following tasks. Use the advice in the column on the right to complete it.

1 Holiday magazine

Holiday Now is a free magazine, which is available at travel agents and other outlets, so it is read by people thinking of booking holidays. The Editor has asked you to write a short article:

'… a special issue about holidays for children. I want you to tell the readers the kinds of activity that are offered – and focus on the 'fun' element in these holidays.'

2 Female magazine

Women Today is a lively magazine for women: it is read both by women in paid employment and by those at home with young families. The Editor has asked you to write about adventure holidays for children:

'A lot of our readers are thinking about separate holidays for children, but they're worried about issues like, "Isn't seven or eight rather young for them to go on holiday on their own?" "Will they enjoy it?" Above all they want to know, "Is it safe?"

3 Leaflet

PGL is planning to produce a leaflet to be slipped into holiday magazines. The Promotions Manager has asked you to plan it:

'We want as many pictures as possible, but we've also got to get the message across in words. Remember the key words: fun, adventure, safety.'

1 Pre-planning

Think about the information you need to collect. (You may like to make a short list.)

2 Research

Read the text again and find the information you need. Write it down. If you need quotations, write them down.

3 Pictures

Decide which pictures you wish to use. You should choose at least two and not more than four.

4 Planning

Decide on the order in which you want to present the information.

5 First draft

Write the first draft. Include a caption for each of the pictures.

6 Taking advice

Ask someone else to read what you have written and comment on it. Don't worry about small details – focus on what you have said and how you have said it.

7 Final draft

Now write your final draft. When you have finished, check your work carefully.

Explaining abseiling TF

The words and pictures on pages 12 and 13 give you a great deal of information about abseiling and why people at PGL think it is a good idea for people to try it. They don't actually explain *what* it is or *how* you do it.

1 Study the material carefully. Try to get a clear idea of how you abseil.
2 Make a list of what you do and the order in which you do it. Remember that there are two people involved, not one:

   ■ the abseiler
   ■ the instructor on the safety rope.

1 The instructor goes up the tower.
2 He attaches the safety rope to the tower.
3 The abseiler puts on the harness.
4 She goes up the tower.

3 Write a clear explanation of how it works. When you do this, try to avoid over-using the words *and* and *then*:

The instructor goes up the tower **and then** he attaches the safety rope **and then** the abseiler puts on the harness **and then** she goes up the tower.

There are other ways in which you can link the phrases:

The instructor goes up the tower **and attaches** the safety rope to the tower. **When** the abseiler **has put** on the harness she goes up the tower.

These are some of the words you could use:

when	after	before
then	while	

4 When you have finished, ask someone else to read what you have written and comment on it.
5 Make any changes needed.

Speech and writing TF

The text on pages 9–14 is not exactly what the two people said. We have edited it to make it easier to read. You can see what we have done from these two extracts:

Tape

normal day would start with wake up which is huh anything from sort of seven seven fifteen in the morning we're the ones that run round and tell them to wake up make sure everyone is ok they'll make sure they've all slept ok this that and the other sometimes it's make sure they go for a wash give them a shower make sure they're going to do their teeth and things then get them through breakfast.

Printed version

A normal day would start with Wake Up which is 7–7.15 in the morning. We're the ones that run round and tell them to wake up [and] make sure everyone is OK. We make sure they go for a wash, give them a shower, [and] make sure they're going to do their teeth. Then [we] get them through breakfast.

What changes?

1 Look carefully at the two texts. Make a list of the changes that have been made.
2 What is the effect of each of these changes?

You try

The extract that follows comes from one of the interviews, but was not used in the printed version. Edit it and write it out so that it can be read easily.

OK they get back about half four possibly five o'clock then they've got to clean themselves up many of them just want to kick the ball round a game of football so we're out there organising games making sure everybody's happy some of them just want to sit and write a postcard home that sort of thing get them through dinner and once they're through dinner it's the dreaded tuck shop time its er get the pocket money out and off they go to the tuck shop you've got to keep an eye on them make sure they're not eating too much chocolate huh erm that sort of thing then into the evening which is their evening activities which is possibly the third activity of the day its a its a full drawn up evening programme of events

Castaway EXT

For some people, the idea of being cast away on a desert island sounds like a real adventure. The reality can be rather different.

In 1703 Alexander Selkirk was the ship's first mate on an expedition to South America. While the ship was anchored off an island off the coast of Chile, he fell out with the Captain and refused to go any further. He demanded to be put ashore on the island and the ship sailed without him.

Five years later, another ship stopped at the island to take on water and supplies. The crew was amazed to discover a strange figure dressed in goats' skins. It was Alexander Selkirk. This is how the captain described Selkirk's ordeal:

He had with him his Clothes and Bedding, with a Fire-lock, some Powder, Bullets, and Tobacco, a Hatchet, a Knife, a Kettle, a Bible, some practical Pieces, and his Mathematical Instruments and Books. He diverted and provided for himself as well as he could; but for the first eight months had much ado to bear up against Melancholy, and the Terror of being left alone in such a desolate place. He built two Hutts with Piemento Trees, cover'd them with long Grass, and lin'd them with the Skins of Goats, which he kill'd with his Gun as he wanted, so long as his Powder lasted, which was but a pound; and that being near spent, he got fire by rubbing two sticks of Piemento Wood together upon his knee.

10

In the lesser Hutt, at some distance from the other, he dress'd his Victuals, and in the larger he slept, and employ'd himself in reading, singing Psalms, and praying; so that he said he was a better Christian while in this Solitude than ever he was before, or than, he was afraid, he should ever be again. At first he never eat anything till Hunger constrain'd him, partly for grief and partly for want of Bread and Salt; nor did he go to bed till he could watch no longer: the Piemento Wood, which burnt very clear, serv'd him both for Firing and Candle, and refresh'd him with its fragrant Smell.

He might have had fish enough, but could not eat 'em for want of Salt, because they occasion'd a Looseness; except Crawfish, which are there as large Lobsters, and very good: These he sometimes broil'd, and at other times boil'd, as he did his Goats Flesh, of which he made very good Broth, for they are not so rank as ours: he kept an Account of 500 that he kill'd while there, and caught as many more, which he mark'd on the ear and let go. When his Powder fail'd, he took them by speed of foot; for his way of living and continual Exercise of walking and running, clear'd him of all gross Humours, so that he ran with wonderful Swiftness thro the Woods and up the Rocks and Hills, as we perceiv'd when we employ'd him to catch Goats for us. We had a Bull-Dog, which we sent with several of our nimblest Runners to help him in catching Goats; but he distanc'd and tir'd both Dog and the Men, catch'd the Goats, and brought 'em to us on his back. He told us that his Agility in pursuing a Goat had once like to have cost him his Life; he pursu'd it with so much Eagerness that he catch'd hold of it on the brink of a Precipice, of which he was not aware, the Bushes having hid it from him; so that he fell with the Goat down the said Precipice a great height, and was so stunn'd and bruised with the Fall, that he narrowly escap'd with his Life, and when he came to his Senses, found the Goat dead under him. He lay there about 24 hours, and was scarce able to crawl to his Hutt, which was about a mile distant, or to stir abroad in ten days.

He soon wore out all his Shoes and Clothes by running thro the Woods; and at last being forc'd to shift without them, his Feet became so hard, that he run everywhere without Annoyance: and it was some time before he could wear Shoes after we found him; for not being us'd to any so long, his Feet swell'd when he came first to wear 'em again.

After he had conquer'd his Melancholy, he diverted himself sometimes by cutting his Name on Trees, and the Time of his being left and Continuance there. He was at first much pester'd with Cats and Rats, that had bred in great numbers from some of each Species which had got ashore from Ships and put in there to wood and water. The Rats gnaw'd his Feet and Clothes while asleep, which oblig'd him to cherish the Cats with his Goats-flesh; by which many of them became so tame, that they would lie about him in hundreds, and soon deliver'd him from the Rats. He likewise tamed some Kids, and to divert himself would now and then sing and dance with them and his Cats: so that by the Care of Providence and Vigour of his

Youth, being now but about 30 years old, he came at last to conquer all the Inconveniences of his Solitude, and to be very easy. When his Clothes wore out, he made himself a Coat and Cap of Goat-Skins which he stitch'd together with little Thongs of the same, that he cut with his Knife. He had no other Needle but a Nail; and when his Knife was wore to the back, he made others as well as he could of some Iron Hoops that were left ashore, which he beat thin and ground upon Stones. Having some Linen Cloth by him, he sow'd himself Shirts with a Nail, and stitch'd 'em with the Worsted of his old Stockings, which he pull'd out on purpose. He had his last Shirt on when we found him on the Island.

Captain Woodes Rogers: *A cruising voyage round the world*

TF Questions

Each of these questions is quite broad. Before writing an answer, you will need to look carefully at the text and collect all the necessary information.

1 When Selkirk went ashore he took some equipment with him. Why did he choose the things he did? How useful do you think he found them?
2 What early problems did he encounter and how did he overcome them? (Careful – they are not all at the beginning of the passage!)
3 What evidence is there that he was a resourceful man?
4 What picture do you get of his way of life, once he had overcome the early problems?
5 What overall impression do you get of Selkirk as a person?

Interview

If Selkirk had lived today he would have been overwhelmed by the media on his return home. Imagine that TV and radio had existed then. Selkirk is interviewed and appears on chat shows. Choose one radio or TV programme on which he appears. Write an account of the event.
Either:
■ as a story
Or
■ as a script.

Marketing the castaway

Today, a popular hero – such as Selkirk would be – is often approached by companies wishing to use a famous name to market goods, as happens with sports personalities. Think of a list of products that could have the 'Selkirk Brand Image' applied to them and describe how they might be marketed.

Words

Daring – good or bad?

All the words in this list have similar meanings, but they do not mean exactly the same.

audacious   fearless   hasty   imprudent   rash
bold   foolhardy   hotheaded   madcap   reckless
courageous   game   impetuous   pioneering   venturesome
daring   hardy

1 Choose four of them. For each one write a sentence using it correctly. Make up sentences that show clearly the differences in the meanings of the words.
2 Some of the words are normally used to express approval (like 'courageous') while others express disapproval (like 'rash'). Others may be neutral, showing neither approval nor disapproval. Write them out in three columns:

approval	neutral	disapproval

Wordpower

All these words are in the unit you have been reading.

1 Explain the meaning of as many as you can.
2 For those you cannot explain, find them in the unit and try to work out their meaning from the sentence they are in.
3 For any that are left, look them up in a dictionary.
4 Make sure you can spell them all.

word	page	line	word	page	line	word	page	line
assault	10	39	aspect(s)	10	38	melancholy	18	7
kayak	10	42	element	12	86	solitude	19	17
capsize(s)	10	53	don(ned)	12	97	fragrant	19	22
interval(s)	11	64	technique(s)	13	104	cherish	19	54
angle	13	106	competent	13	110	inconvenience(s)	20	60

Star quality

What is a star?

What comes into your mind when you hear people talk about 'stars' or 'star quality'?

- Is it a particular kind of work?
- Or is it, perhaps, something to do with personality?
- Or is it just luck?

Make a list of stars you can think of and try to work out if they have anything in common.

A star is born

You are going to create a star.
All you need is one ordinary human being.

1 Choose someone from your class, your friends or your family who you think deserves to be transformed.
2 Now decide what kind of star they are going to be.

   Think about the possibilities…

model, soccer player, singer, actor, rock guitarist, politician, athlete, motorcyclist, agony columnist, royalty, tennis player, swimmer, television personality, rugby player, writer, disc jockey, dancer, company director, film star, racing driver…

3 Now think about your chosen person. Choose two or three possible star careers for them. For each career make notes about the qualities needed to become a star.

> Politician
> must be good speaker
> should not be easily rattled
>
> Tennis player
> needs excellent co-ordination
> must like travel

4 Look at your notes and decide which career most suits your chosen person.
5 Now write a short account of what you have decided. Include these points:

   ■ who you have chosen
   ■ the star career you have selected for them
   ■ why you have chosen it.

> I have chosen Alison to be a star politician because she loves getting up and talking to the rest of the class and she never seems the slightest bit nervous. Also I think

Lifestyle

A star needs a lifestyle that goes with being famous. So it's out with that old wardrobe of clothes and in with a brand-new look.

tucks and darts

pearls

Gearing up

1 For the star you are creating, write some notes about:

- everyday clothes and shoes
- outfits for special occasions
- hair
- make-up
- general style.

> – wears dyed purple fake fur coat
> – perfume by Calvin Klein (Escape)
> – chooses Gucci T-shirts for wearing at home

2 Write a description of the look of the star you are creating and illustrate your description where appropriate.

> Tania is tall and often wears black leggings under a long coat which emphasises her height. Her dark eyes are matched by her black hair which is shoulder-length and lightly permed.

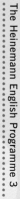

A special kind of home

Home for a star

Think about what kind of home would be suitable for your star. Would your star have more than one home? Create the kind of home (or homes) that you think your star would live in.

1 Make notes on:

   ■ the type of house
   ■ where it would be situated
   ■ how it would be decorated
   ■ its special features and facilities.

2 Describe and illustrate the home(s) of the star you are creating.

All in a day's work

You don't become a star by sitting around all day doing nothing. Up-and-coming stars are busy people with hectic schedules … people to see, diets to keep to, training to complete, interviews to give, work to be done.

0800   Breakfast meeting with tour manager
       (here)

1000   Olympic studios booked to listen to
       overdubs
       (We need to leave here by 0930 at latest)

1230   Workout session booked as requested at
       O'Casey's
       (If studio session looks likely to overrun
       we can cancel but we must tell them by
       1200 – they are doing us a favour.)

1415   LBC interview re. forthcoming tour and
       the Hammersmith Odeon ban
       (Need to leave O'Casey's by about 1330
       and grab a sandwich en route. Notes for
       LBC interview attached.)

The schedule

1 Make notes on the things that your star
   might do in the course of a busy day.
2 Turn your notes into a schedule like the
   one above.

A day in the life

3 Now describe your star's day. Write as if
   you were one of these people:

   ■ the star
   ■ the star's personal assistant or
     secretary
   ■ the star's bodyguard.

Making the headlines

Newspapers and magazines need stars to make their headlines.
Stars need headlines in order to stay famous.

What do they want to know?

What do you think a magazine might want to know about the stars?

1   Make a list of the questions a journalist might want to ask your star. Here are some possibilities:

- their background – childhood, schooling, how they got started
- what they've achieved – mainly factual
- how they feel about their achievements
- how they live today – their home, a typical day's work
- how they cope with success
- personal gossip
- the highs and the lows.

What does the star tell them?

2   Think about how your star might answer the questions. Make notes on each question.

The article

3   Now write the article, using the notes you have made.

A rhyme sometime

Page	Title	What you do	Why you do it
33–35	**On and on...**	Read a poem by Roger McGough and think about how it works. Play with words following the pattern in the poem. Add further verses to the poem.	To start you thinking about the themes of the unit. To get you to think carefully about the language used in poems. To develop your imagination.
36–37	**Animal instincts**	Read three poems which describe people as if they were different animals and discuss which of the poems you prefer and why. Write your own poem in which someone you know well is described as if they were an animal.	To continue to develop your imagination and skills as a writer.
38–39	**Sister in a whale**	Read the poem and then think about it and answer the questions. Write a description of your room (or someone's that you know). Try using the poetic techniques listed.	To continue to develop your imagination and skills as a writer.
40	**What's happened?**	Compare two pictures and note the differences. Look at some of the words you used.	To get you looking closely and making notes. To begin to learn about prepositions.
41	**Prepositions**	Look at the sentences you wrote, and study the ways in which they were constructed.	To understand more about language by learning about prepositions and prepositional phrases.
42–43	**Stopping to think**	Read a poem and discuss ways of describing it.	To develop your ability to talk and write about literature.
44–45	**The river's story**	Read the poem and answer questions about it. Write your own poem following a similar pattern.	To develop your ability to talk and write about a poem in detail. To give you an opportunity to develop your own ideas in writing.
46–47	**Let me in**	Read a poem that has a story hidden in it. Work in a group to develop your ideas about the story and the poem. Study the poem in detail.	To develop your ability to talk and write about a poem in detail.
48–49	**Punctuating poetry Wordpower**	Look at a poem and think how it should be punctuated. Compare your version with the way the poet did it. Do a spelling quiz and look at words used in the unit.	To get you thinking carefully about punctuation. To develop your vocabulary and your spelling.

A *rhyme sometime*

Poetry comes dressed in a whole range of clothes: humorous, serious, rhyming, narrative, descriptive, rhythmic, mysterious ... and everyone has their favourites. This unit gives you a chance to look at a range of very different poems, to think about them, to respond to them and to write in a range of ways including poetry itself.

On and on ...

Is a well-wisher
    someone
who wishes at a well?

Is a bad speller
    one
who casts a wicked spell?

Is a shop-lifter
    a giant
who goes around lifting shops?

10   Is a pop singer
    someone
who sings and then pops?

Is a fly fisherman
    an angler
who fishes for flies?

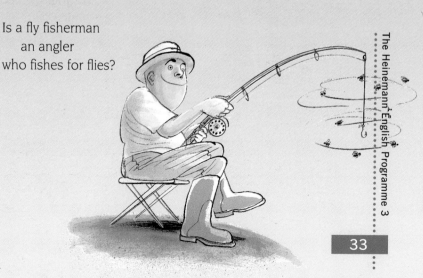

Is an eye-opener
    a gadget
for opening eyes?

Is a night nurse
    a nurse
who looks after the night?

Who puts it to bed
    and then
turns off the light?

Is a big spender
    a spendthrift
who is exceedingly big?

Is a pig farmer
    really
a land-owning pig?

Does a baby-sitter
    really
sit on tiny tots?

Is a pot-holer
    a gunman
who shoots holes in pots?

Roger McGough

Poetry as wordplay

Hundreds of words and phrases in English can have more than one meaning. Roger McGough has taken well-known words and phrases and given them a new twist.

Think up new definitions for some of the people and things in the box below. Don't worry about turning them into a rhyming poem. Concentrate on playing with the words and having fun with the definition. Like this:

headteacher
a person who teaches pupils who have heads (and hence brains). In the old days pupils were often sent to school without their heads and these children were always taught by the assistant teachers rather than the headteachers. Over a period of time, the headteachers came to be seen as the senior teachers and eventually as the person in charge of the school.

Try some of these

a grandmother	a disc jockey	homework	TF
a wardrobe	a film star	a merry-go-round	
a kitchen table	bubble bath	a head cold	
a wristwatch	an alarm clock	a flypaper	
a caretaker	double glazing	a gamekeeper	

The pattern

The verses in Roger McGough's poem follow similar patterns.

1 Which things are the same in every verse?
2 Choose the two verses that you think have the most similar construction. Explain why they are so alike.
3 Choose one verse that is different from the rest in some way. Explain the difference.
4 How does the poem rhyme?

Further verses

Roger McGough's poem is the sort you can keep on adding verses to as you think of them.

How might you finish off an extra verse such as this one?

> Is a silkworm
>   a worm
> who _____?

Use the patterns of the poem to create verses of your own.

> Is a _____
>   a _____
> who _____?

Animal instincts

These poems were written by Alex Wills when he was a pupil at St George's School in Hong Kong.

The horse

Cantering
Up and down the field
Whinnying his orders
'Twenty press ups,
Ten sit ups,
Twenty squat thrusts
Twenty tuck jumps.
Now!
And remember,
10   I'll be watching you.'
He neighs
'You Smith
You only did nine and
Must do ten more
Because Smith cheated.
'Smith,
Come to my stall after
Now everyone
Gallop twenty furlongs
20   Quickly.'

The budgie

Fluttering helplessly around
A cage of ignorance
The 1st year Set 4 teacher
Struggles to educate her charges,
In the rudiments of reading and writing.
Banging her head against
The tinkling mirror
Of their witlessness
She holds herself in check,
10   Telling herself not to peck them
Or to squawk at them
But
To tell them
Quietly and calmly
TO GET ON WITH THEIR WORK.

The wolf

Standing at the front of the classroom
He is in perfect control.
Occasionally he pads around the room.
The class is silent
Except for the scratch of pens on paper.
About halfway through the lesson
There is a whisper
From the back of the room
And
He turns his gaze towards its source
Transfixing the child
With his strange lupine stare
And the pupil is still.
The room is now like a morgue
But a morgue with strangely industrious
Corpses.

Discussion

■ Which line or lines do you like best in each poem?
   What do you like about those lines?
■ Which poem do you prefer? Why?

Writing

Write your own poem in which someone you know well
is described as if they were an animal. You can choose
an adult or a young person. Remember that they may
see the poem!

TF

Sister in a whale

You live in the hollow of a stranded whale
lying on top of our house.
My father was embarrassed by this
so a roof was put up as camouflage.
On the ribs you have hung plants
and a miniature replica of a whale
to remind you where you are.
The stomach lining is plastered with posters
and your Snoopy for President buttons
10   are stuck to a piece of blubber beside your bed.
Through the spout you observe cloud formations.
It isn't as orderly as a regular room:
it's more like a shipwreck of notebooks,
school projects, shirts, paper bags,
coke cans, photographs and magazines
that has been washed up with the tide.
You beachcomb every morning for something to wear;
then it's down the corkscrew
to the real world.

Julie O'Callaghan

Thinking about the poem

1 What do you think would be your impression of this bedroom as you came through the door?
2 Which part of the description do you like best?
3 Different parts of the whale are mentioned:

   ribs
   stomach lining
   piece of blubber
   spout

   How does each of these link with the bedroom?
4 What else is unusual about the description?
5 This sister's room is compared to the inside of a whale in an **extended metaphor.** What other things could be compared to a bedroom?

My room

Write a description of your own room (or your brother's/sister's/friend's room).
Try to compare it with something else in the way that Julie O'Callaghan has done.

Literary terms

alliteration
where two or more closely connected words begin with the same sound.
An example from the poem is:
   blubber beside your bed
■ find another example of alliteration from 'Sister in a whale'.

simile
a comparison in which one thing is said to be similar to another. An example from the poem is the description of the room as:
   more like a shipwreck of notebooks
■ find another example of a simile from 'The wolf' on page 37.

metaphor
Instead of saying something is *like* something else, it is described as if it were *actually* that thing. In the poem, the sister's bedroom becomes the inside of the whale:
   You live in the hollow of a stranded whale
   lying on top of our house
■ find another example of a metaphor from 'Sister in a whale'.

What's happened?

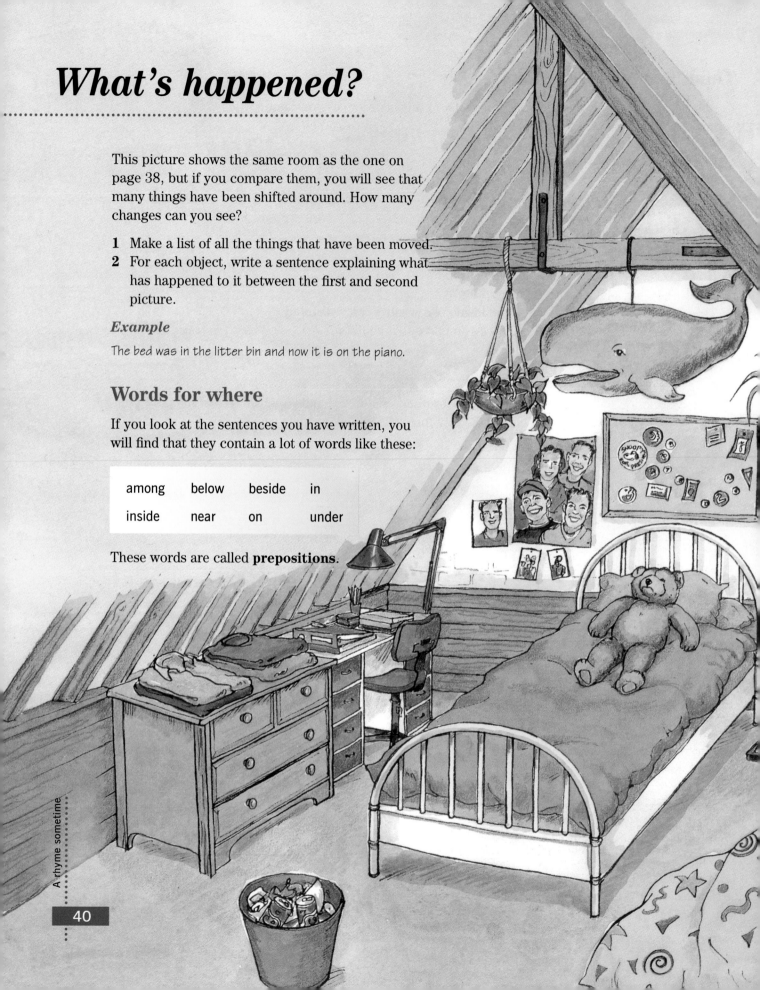

This picture shows the same room as the one on page 38, but if you compare them, you will see that many things have been shifted around. How many changes can you see?

1 Make a list of all the things that have been moved.
2 For each object, write a sentence explaining what has happened to it between the first and second picture.

Example

The bed was in the litter bin and now it is on the piano.

Words for where

If you look at the sentences you have written, you will find that they contain a lot of words like these:

among	below	beside	in
inside	near	on	under

These words are called **prepositions**.

Prepositions

Prepositions are some of the commonest 'little words' in English. They are used with nouns to make a group of words called a **prepositional phrase**. They often tell us about *where* something is or where something happens:

The bed was **in** *the litter bin* *and now it is* **on** *the piano* *.*

That put the cat **among** *the pigeons* *.*

Which prepositions did you use?

1 Look at the sentences you wrote for number 2 on the opposite page. Underline the prepositions you used.
2 Look at the list in the box on the opposite page. Choose four prepositions and write a sentence for each one, using it correctly.

The prepositions you have been using consist of **one** word. But a preposition can also be a small group of words. For example:

■ next to
■ on top of

Precisely speaking

English has many prepositions and some of them are very similar in meaning. So you may have a choice of prepositions. For example:

■ next to   beside   alongside
■ above   on top of   over

What is the difference between the prepositions in each of those groups? How would you use each one?

TF

Other meanings for prepositional phrases

So far we have been looking at phrases that tell us about **where**. But prepositional phrases can also answer other questions. Match up the two columns:

Sentence with prepositional phrase (in bold)	Question the phrase answers
They usually go to football matches **by bus**.	When? / How long?
She wasn't allowed to go out **because of the mess in her room**.	How? / In what way?
I can hold my breath **for more than ninety seconds**.	Why? / For what purpose?

If you ask poets why they wrote a particular poem, they will give you many different answers. One reason may be that they wanted to make people stop and think. That might well be what Philip Larkin would have told you about this poem.

Take one home for the kiddies

On shallow straw, in shadeless glass,
Huddled by empty bowls, they sleep:
No dark, no dam, no earth, no grass –
Mam, get us one of them to keep.

Living toys are something novel
But it soon wears off somehow.
Fetch the shoebox, fetch the shovel –
Mam, we're playing funerals now.

Philip Larkin

dam: mother

A rhyme sometime

Is it true?

Look at these statements about the poem.

A

The pets are well looked after in the pet shop.

B

The children have a deep love of animals.

C

The children do not understand about the needs of animals.

D

The pets are treated more like packets of biscuits than living creatures.

1 Decide whether you think they are true or false.
2 What evidence or reason can you find for your opinion?
3 Make a record of your decisions and reasons:

Statement	✔ or ✘	Reasons
A	✘	They haven't got enough straw ('on shallow straw') They're probably too hot, because

The poem is about . . .

Look at these four opinions of what the poem is about.

E

This is a poem about the evils of pet shops.

F

This is a poem about human carelessness.

G

This is a poem about cruelty to animals.

H

This is a poem about how adults spoil children.

1 Try to put the four statements in order, starting with the best description of the poem at number one and finishing with the weakest at number four.
2 Write the statements in that order on a piece of paper.
3 Beside each one explain what you think of it as an opinion about the poem and why.
4 Can you think of one or more statements of your own to describe what the poem is doing?

The river's story

I remember when life was good.
I shilly-shallied across meadows,
Tumbled down mountains,
I laughed and gurgled through woods,
Stretched and yawned in a myriad of floods.
Insects, weightless as sunbeams,
Settled upon my skin to drink.
I wore lily-pads like medals.
Fish, lazy and battle-scarred,
10   Gossiped beneath them.
    The damselflies were my ballerinas,
    The pike my ambassadors.
     Kingfishers, disguised as rainbows,
     Were my secret agents.
     It was a sweet time, a gone-time,
    A time before factories grew,
    Brick by greedy brick,
    And left me cowering
    In monstrous shadows.
20   Like drunken giants
   They vomited their poisons into me.
Tonight a scattering of vagrant bluebells,
Dwarfed by those same poisons,
Toll my ending.
Children, come and find me if you wish,
I am your inheritance.
Behind the derelict housing-estates
  You will discover my remnants.
   Clogged with garbage and junk
30   To an open sewer I've shrunk.
   I, who have flowed through history,
    Who have seen hamlets become villages,
     Villages become towns, towns become cities,
    Am reduced to a trickle of filth
    Beneath the still, burning stars.

Brian Patten

Understanding the poem

1 Which of these statements gives you the best picture of
the poem and why?

- The poem describes a river.
- The poem describes life in the river.
- The poem describes how a river has been ruined by
pollution.
- The poem describes changes in a river.

2 Find the words in the poem which tell you most clearly:

- what life was like in the past
- what the river is like today.

3 The poet uses imagery to help you imagine what the river
is like. Imagery involves one thing being compared with
something else. (There is more about this on page 39.)
Think about these two comparisons:

- Why might the lily-pads on the river be 'like medals'?
- Why might the river describe the damselflies as 'my
ballerinas'?

4 Look at how the factories are described. What do you
think the poet wants to communicate by this description?

5 The river invites the children to 'come and find me'. Why
do you think it is the children who are invited?

6 The poem is written as if the river is speaking. What
difference does this make to the effect?

7 Write about the contrasts in the poem between the past
and the present, in the form of a table. Use two headings
Past and Present.

8 When you have completed the table write your findings in
a paragraph.

9 Which 'pictures in words' do you think are best? Why?

Past	Present
good	poisoned
river 'laughed' and 'gurgled'	it is like 'an open sewer'

My own poem

1 Think of a place you know that has changed.
2 Try to remember what it used to be like.
3 Think about what it is like now.
4 Imagine that *you* are the place that has
changed.
5 Write about your life as that place and how
things have changed.

Here are some examples of places you could
choose:

- a ruined building
- a disused piece of wasteground that has been
turned into a playground
- fields that have been covered by a housing
estate
- an empty shop.

Let me in

Mary Coleridge, born in 1861, wrote most of her poetry in the last two decades of the nineteenth century. Her poems did not appear in book form until 1907, after her death. This is one of her best-known poems:

I have walked a great while over the snow,
And I am not tall or strong.
My clothes are wet, and my teeth are set,
And the way was hard and long.
I have wandered over the fruitful earth,
But I never came here before.
Oh, lift me over the threshold, and let me in
at the door!

10 The cutting wind is a cruel foe.
I dare not stand in the blast.
My hands are stone, and my voice a groan,
And the worst of death is past.
I am but a little maiden still,
My little white feet are sore.
Oh, lift me over the threshold, and let me in
at the door!

Group work

1 What is your impression of the person who is asking to be let in?
2 Look at the four illustrations of the figure on these pages and decide how close they are to the figure described in the poem.
3 Choose the one that you think best fits the poem and explain how you reached your decision.

Thinking about the poem

Verse One
1 How long has the figure at the door been walking?
2 What has the weather been like?
3 What does the figure at the door say that she looks like?

Verse Two
4 How is the wind described?
5 What else do we discover about what the figure at the door looks like?

Verse Three
6 Describe the voice of the figure at the door in your own words.
7 Why do you think the fire dies when the figure is let into the house?

Her voice was the voice that women have,
Who plead for their heart's desire.
She came – she came – and the quivering flame
Sank and died in the fire.
It never was lit again on my hearth
Since I hurried across the floor,
To lift her over the threshold, and let her in at the door.

Mary Coleridge

Close reading

1 Look at the first verse. How does the figure at the door try to get sympathy?
2 Look again at the first verse. What do you think the figure means by 'my teeth are set'?
3 Look at the second verse. Is there anything here that would increase sympathy for the stranger at the door?
4 Look again at the second verse. What clues are there that the figure at the door may not be an ordinary human being?

5 Look at the third verse. What do you think is happening here? Think about the fire that dies and is never lit again.
6 This poem has a regular rhyme pattern. Can you spot it? (It includes rhymes that are not simply at the end of lines.)
7 Why do you think the figure asks the person to 'lift her over the threshold'? Why not simply ask the person to open the door?
8 Choose a title for the poem and explain your choice.

Punctuating poetry

Punctuating poetry can be a problem. Some poets punctuate in great detail. Others choose to let the line endings create the pauses and add in very little else. Punctuation normally exists to make the meaning clearer. This is not always what the poet is interested in. Sometimes a poet will want readers to work out the meanings for themselves or even to see two meanings.

How would you punctuate this poem?

The horse

cantering
up and down the field
whinnying his orders
twenty press ups
ten sit ups
twenty squat thrusts
twenty tuck jumps
now
and remember
ill be watching you
he neighs
you smith
you only did nine and
must do ten more
because smith cheated
smith
come to my stall after
now everyone
gallop twenty furlongs
quickly

1 Look at 'The horse' and decide what punctuation it needs.
2 Now compare your punctuation with the poet's punctuation, which you can find earlier in the unit on page 36.
3 Can you see any places where the poet has not followed the normal patterns of punctuation?
4 Are there any places where you have not followed the normal punctuation patterns?
5 How helpful do you think your punctuation of the poem is?

Spelling quiz

All the words in this quiz occur somewhere in this unit. Work out what the word is and write it out with the correct spelling.
Note: each blank can be one letter or more than one.

1 To O–ERVE is to look at or study something.
2 C–M–FL–GE is how animals conceal themselves.
3 A SH–P–E–K can happen when a boat is caught in a storm.
4 If my mother kisses me in public, I am E–BAR–S–ED.
5 It doesn't happen often, it happens OC–ONA–.
6 S–UA–K is the loud noise of an angry bird.
7 I–N–R–N–E is a lack of knowledge.
8 A small bell can make a T–NK–ING sound.
9 CO–P–ES are dead bodies.
10 If you are hard-working, you are IND–ST–US.

Wordpower

All these words are in the unit you have been reading.

1 Explain the meaning of as many as you can.
2 For those you cannot explain, find them in the unit and try to work out their meaning from the sentence they are in.
3 For any that are left, look them up in a dictionary.
4 Make sure you can spell them all.

word	page	line	word	page	line	word	page	line
peck	36	10	fluttering	36	1	rudiments	36	5
spout	38	11	industrious	37	15	witlessness	36	8
corkscrew	38	18	blubber	38	10	transfixing	37	11
funerals	42	8	beachcomb	38	17	lupine	37	12
ballerina(s)	44	11	huddled	42	2	morgue	37	14
blast	46	10	monstrous	44	19	replica	38	6
quivering	47	19	vagrant	44	22	threshold	46	7

It's fantastic!

It's fantastic!

First impressions

On pages 52–56 you will find the opening scene of a play. This picture shows the scene as the play begins. **Before you start to read the script**, look carefully at the illustration.

■ What strikes you most about the house?
■ Who do you think the man in the living room is and what is your impression of him?
■ What impression do you get of the woman in the kitchen?
■ What about the boy in the bedroom?
■ The other bedroom is empty. What kind of person do you think it belongs to?

LUCY *now appears from along the street, carrying her school bag.*
She stops as she reaches her house. Faint traffic and perhaps a little
urban birdsong.

LUCY: (*To the audience*) It all started the Friday I came home from school
to tell my family some exciting news. By the way, my name's Lucy
Baines. That's my mother there in the kitchen. And my father
pretending he's watching the telly but actually he's fast asleep. And
that one upstairs, that's my older brother – known usually as Grisly
Gary. Anyway, you'll meet them soon enough because unfortunately
they all feature in this story I'm going to tell you. As soon as you
have met them, you're immediately going to wish you hadn't met
them. I mean, they're all right. I suppose. Sometimes. Very, very,
very occasionally. Like every fifth Christmas in June, they're all
right. It's not that they're cruel to me or anything. I think they
actually do love me, really, though you'd never know it most of the
time. They're just so – gloomy and glum. Like you know that saying:
'Eat, Drink and Be Merry for Tomorrow We Die'? Well, my Dad's
version of that is, 'Tomorrow We Die, So What Are You Looking So
Cheerful About?' I mean, I don't expect them to leap about laughing
all day long but, well, on a day like this for instance, when I came
home on this particular Friday with this terrific news – it would have
been nice to have had a really warm welcome.

(*She goes through the front door.*)

(*Calling as she goes*) Mum! Mum!

JOY: (*Immensely cheerily*) Lucy, you're home at last! How lovely to see
you!

LUCY: Hallo, Mum.

(*They embrace.*)

JOY: Oh, you're looking so bonny. Have you had a good day at school?
Tell me all about it.

LUCY: Wonderful, I've had a wonderful day. I have to tell you, Mum, it's so
exciting – I've been chosen for the school swimming team.

JOY: (*With a cry of delight*) You haven't!

LUCY: I have! The relay and the 200 metres backstroke.

JOY: Backstroke! Oh, that's just wonderful. We must tell your Dad. Dad!

LUCY: Oh, don't wake him up.

JOY: No, I must. He'll want to know. Walt! Walter!

WALT: (*Waking up cheerfully*) What's that? What's all this?

JOY: Dad, listen to this, listen to this news.

WALT: (*Playfully*) Did I doze off ? I must have dozed off.

JOY: (*Affectionately*) Yes, you did, you know you did, you old devil. And
now you're awake you can just listen to Lucy's news.

WALT: News? What news is this? Come on, out with it, young Lucy.

JOY: Tell him your news.

LUCY: I will when you'll let me get a word in. Dad, I've been picked for the school swimming team.

(WALT *stares at her, speechless.*)

(*Shrugging modestly*) That's all.

WALT: The school swimming team?

50 LUCY: Yes.

JOY: Backstroke and relay.

WALT: (*Rather overcome*) Backstroke and relay?

LUCY: Yes.

(WALT *moves to* LUCY *and hugs her fiercely. He is obviously deeply moved.*)

WALT: I'm so proud, girl. I'm so proud of you. This is the proudest day of my life.

JOY: And mine, Dad. And mine.

WALT: Where's that lad Gary, then? We must tell Gary.

60 JOY: Oh, yes. We must tell Gary. (*Calling*) Gary!

WALT: (*Calling*) Gary!

(GARY, *at the sound of their voices, springs off his bed and starts downstairs eagerly.*)

LUCY: Oh, don't disturb him.

JOY: No, he'll want to know.

WALT: The lad'll want to know.

JOY: (*Calling*) Gary!

WALT: (*Calling*) Gary!

Questions

1 What is Lucy's opinion of her family?

2 What has happened to her that day?

3 How do her mother and father react to her news in this scene?

4 How do we know that this is not what really happened?

GARY: (*Having come downstairs*) Yes? What is it? (*Overjoyed*) Hallo,
70   Lucy! Are you home from school already?

LUCY: Hi, Gary.

GARY: Did somebody call? What can I do for you?

JOY: Tell him your news, then.

WALT: Tell him your news.

LUCY: I've been picked for the school swimming team.

JOY: Two hundred metres backstroke…

WALT: And the relay.

(*A fractional pause, then* GARY *steps forward, picks up* LUCY *and whirls her in his arms.*)

80 GARY: (*As he does this*) YIPPEEE !

(*A huge crowd starts cheering.*)

JOY: Hooray!

WALT: Bravo!

(*The briefest burst of vigorous brass-band music. Before festivities can get under way,* LUCY *disengages herself from the riotous group and steps back outside the house again. Under the next, the others quietly resume their original starting positions.*)

LUCY: (*As she moves*) I mean, I didn't expect them to behave quite like
        that. But, you know, they could have at least said 'good' or
90   something. 'Well done', even. But anyway, on this particular day, I
        came home from school – this is my house by the way – Number
        162 Sycamore Street – it's just past the traffic lights and before you
        get to the zebra crossing, I don't know if you know Sycamore Street
        at all but – (*Breaking off again*) Sorry, I'm rambling again. On this
        Friday I came home full of excitement, with my fantastic news about
        the school swimming team.

(*As* LUCY *enters the house, the traffic sounds disappear and are replaced by the noises inside. The TV drones on throughout and upstairs, faintly, the thud of* GARY'S *music.*)

100   Mum!

JOY: (*Without stopping her tasks*) Shh! Your father's asleep.

LUCY: (*Whispering*) Sorry! Mum, guess what?

JOY: Your dad's had a terrible day. His van broke down again, miles from
        nowhere …

LUCY: I've got this amazing news…

JOY: … he had to walk five miles…

LUCY: … go on, guess what happened to me today.

JOY: … by the time he'd phoned the AA and then walked five miles all the
        way back again, someone had stolen his front wheels.

110 LUCY: Shall I tell you?

JOY: Left his van standing on six bricks. I mean, I don't know what the
        world's coming to, I really don't.

LUCY: I'll tell you, shall I?

JOY: Stealing people's front wheels. I mean, what if your dad had been a pensioner? What if he'd been disabled …?

LUCY: I've been picked for the school swimming team.

JOY: They should bring in stricter laws and stop all this vandalism in one fell swoop. I mean, the way we're going at the moment, none of us will be able to sleep securely in our beds …

120 LUCY: Two hundred metres backstroke. And the relay.

JOY: I mean, look at old Mrs Hadron. Those lads rode their bike right through her back garden. Ruined her bird table, cut up her lawn …

LUCY: Isn't that great news?

JOY: I mean, they should have been locked up. She's got no husband and her little dog's poorly. You see, if this council worried less about putting up new bandstands and building multi-storey car parks and a little more on making the streets safe from vandals and layabouts.

130 (LUCY *holds a conversation with herself.*)

LUCY: (*Under this last*) 'Tremendous news, Lucy. Absolutely fantastic. You're brilliant, I don't know how you do it …' 'Oh, it was nothing, Mum, really …'

JOY: (*Stopping as she sees* LUCY) What are you going on about there?

Questions

5 How does Joy react when Lucy tries to tell her her news?

6 What has happened to Lucy's dad that day?

7 What impression do you get of Joy from these two pages? (*Think about her name!*)

LUCY: Nothing.

JOY: What were you saying?

LUCY: Nothing. Just talking to myself, Mum. (*Under her breath*) As usual.

JOY: (*Suspiciously*) You haven't got that friend of yours back, have you?

LUCY: What?

JOY: That – invisible friend of yours? I hope you're not starting all that again?

LUCY: No.

JOY: You know how that annoys your dad.

LUCY: Yep.

(*She moves away.*)

JOY: Where're you going?

LUCY: Upstairs. Put my things away.

JOY: Well, come straight down again. It's nearly tea-time. You can give me a hand.

LUCY: Right.

JOY: I've been on my feet all day, I've not had a minute's break since I got up, it's all right for the rest of you … (JOY's *stream of complaining drops to a low mutter as* LUCY *moves out of earshot. She moves to where* WALT *is sitting asleep in front of the TV. As she nears him the TV fades up a little.*)

TV VOICE: And finally … more sobering economic news as the pound slumped lower still against a basket of other currencies. On top of that, inflation, as we heard earlier, is also up and indications are, according to the latest forecasts, that it will rise still further over the next three months. Later on this evening, in Newsnight, we shall be showing a special programme in which seven European economic experts will be giving their verdict: Is Britain's Economy a Sinking Ship? That'll be on Newsnight at 10.30 tonight. But now it's time to go over to Bert Cod at the London Weather Centre for the latest picture.

(LUCY *watches this for all of two seconds and scowls.*)

LUCY: (*To audience*) Even the TV's depressing in our house. We're only allowed to watch the programmes he wants to watch. And they're all dead boring. This is my father. Who's the current *Guinness Book of Records* twenty-four-hour sleeping champion. (*Loudly*) Whey-hey, Dad! !

WALT: (*Snorting awake*)Whah!

LUCY: Sorry, Dad, did I wake you?

WALT: (*Drowsily*) Not just at the moment, love, I want to watch the news.

(*He falls asleep again.*)

Alan Ayckbourn: *Invisible friends*

Pair readings

A lot of the fun in this script is the contrast between Lucy's fantasy of how her family *might* behave and the reality of how they *do* behave. Work with a partner on two short readings (**A** and **B** below) to show this contrast:

A

start: LUCY: (*Calling as she goes*) Mum! Mum! (line 24)
finish: JOY: No, I must. He'll want to know. Walt! Walter! (line 37)

B

start: LUCY: Mum! (line 100)
finish: JOY: …will be able to sleep securely in our beds … (line 119)

What to do

1 Read the two extracts silently on your own. Try to 'hear' them in your head.
2 With your partner talk about how you think they should be read.
3 Practise reading each one.
4 Discuss what you felt about them and how they went and how you could improve them – work on making a strong (and funny) contrast between them.
5 Practise them again.

Character work

We learn about the characters of Joy, Walter and Gary in three ways:

■ what Lucy tells us about them
■ what they say
■ how they behave.

(Some of this information is contained in the picture on page 51.)
Read the script again and collect all the clues you can about each of these characters. Record your ideas on a chart like this:

Character	What we learn	How we learn it
Gary	He is very untidy. He is lazy.	The picture shows that his room is in a mess. It is the middle of the day but he is lying in bed.

I can dream, can't I?

Lucy's family is so dreary that she fantasises about what they might be like – and we see her fantasy acted out.

Discuss

1 What kind of daydreams or fantasies do you have?
2 What aspects of your life would you like to escape from and why?
3 Think about other people's lives. Use a chart like the one below to list as many different problems and escape fantasies as you can.

Problem	Escape fantasy
Quiet shy office worker, who is bossed around and teased by the people she works with	She is a wealthy tycoon with a yacht in the Mediterranean and a luxury villa in Florida

Write TF

Choose one 'escape fantasy' and write a short story describing how it affects the life of the person who has it. You can write about yourself (as 'I') or about someone else (as 'she/he').

Worlds of fantasy

Many people enjoy reading fantasy stories of different kinds.

Covers

Look at these book covers. What can you tell about the story of each book by looking at the cover?

1 What does the picture suggest that the book will be about?
2 What can you work out from the title?
3 Are there any other words on the cover that suggest what the book will be like?
4 Which of the covers do you think is most attractive?
5 Which book has the most interesting title?
6 Which one would you be most interested in reading and why?

Stories

Each of the extracts that follows is the beginning of a story. Read all three and then follow the instructions on page 61.

A

Let the eye of your imagination be a camera.

This is the universe, a glittering ball of galaxies like the ornament on some unimaginable Christmas tree.

Find a galaxy …

Focus

This is a galaxy, swirled like the cream in a cup of coffee, every pinpoint of light a star. Find a star …

Focus

This is a solar system, where planets barrel through the darkness around the central fires of the sun. Some planets hug close, hot enough to melt lead. Some drift far out, where the comets are born.

Find a blue planet …

Focus

This is a planet. Most of it is covered in water. It's called earth.

Terry and Lyn Pratchett: *Wings*

B

'Poor Thula,' said Aneka from her big leather-curtained horse-litter. 'Is your headache any better?'

That, oddly enough, decided me. My headache was definitely her fault. I made some answer, and reined in my horse to let the big litter lurch through the archway into the inn-yard, nodding to her cousin where he sat on his raw-boned bay horse bawling instructions at the pack-drivers. He ignored me.

'Do you go up,' I said to Aneka. 'I'll stable my horse.'

'Gelen says they serve in half an hour,' she said, jumping down in a swirl of embroidered petticoats. I nodded and led my big grey Dester into the stable. Unsaddling and brushing him down with soothing, accustomed movements, I considered the matter.

If she had drugged my wine, it was with a purpose. I could think of two, but dismissed one. I had lived among girls of my own age or younger since I was seven: if she had done it out of sheer mischief, Aneka of all girls would have shown it, by secret smiles and giggles. And yet the other was incredible.

Pat McIntosh: *Falcon's mate*

C

You'll have heard stories, sometimes, of men who have fought and slain dragons. These are all lies. There's no swordsman living ever killed a dragon, though a few swordsmen dead that tried.

On the other hand, I once travelled in company with a fellow who got the name of 'dragon-slayer'.

A riddle? No. I'll tell you.

I was coming from the North back into the South, to civilisation as you may say, when I saw him sitting by the roadside. My first feeling was envy, I admit. He was smart and very clean for someone in the wilds, and he had the South all over him, towns and baths and money. He was crazy, too, because there was gold on his wrists and in one ear. But he had a sharp grey sword, an army sword, so maybe he could defend himself. He was also younger than me, and a great deal prettier, but the last isn't too difficult. I wondered what he'd do when he looked up from his daydream and saw me, tough, dark and sour as a twist of old rope, clopping down on him on my swarthy little horse, ugly as sin, that I love like a daughter.

Janith Lee: *Draco Draco*

The extracts

When you have read each extract carefully, think about these questions:

1 What kind of story do you think each one introduces?
2 What makes you think that?
3 How do you think each might continue?
4 Which would you most enjoy reading and why?

Writing

Either
1 Choose one of the covers on page 59 and write the beginning of the story it might contain.
or
2 Choose one of the extracts and continue the story.

AFRICA

Timbuktu

Kenya

Tanzania

Wilderness
and Wetlands

Zimbabwe

Namibia

South Africa

Travel

I should like to rise and go
Where the golden apples grow;
Where below another sky
Parrot islands anchored lie,
And, watched by cockatoos and goats,
Lonely Crusoes building boats;
Where in sunshine reaching out
Eastern cities, miles about,
Are with mosque and minaret
10   Among sandy gardens set,
And the rich goods from near and far
Hang for sale in the bazaar;
Where the Great Wall round China goes,
And on one side the desert blows,
And with bell and voice and drum,
Cities on the other hum;
Where are forests, hot as fire,
Wide as England, tall as a spire,
Where the knotty crocodile
20   Lies and blinks in the Nile,
And the red flamingo flies
Hunting fish before his eyes;
Where in jungles, near and far,
Man-devouring tigers are,
Lying close and giving ear
Lest the hunt be drawing near,
Or a comer-by be seen

Swinging in a palanquin;
Where among the desert sands
30   Some deserted city stands,
All its children, sweep and prince,
Grown to manhood ages since,
Not a foot in street or house,
Not a stir of child or mouse,
And when kindly falls the night,
In all the town no spark of light.
There I'll come when I'm a man
With a camel caravan;
Light a flower in the gloom
40   Of some dusty dining-room;
See the pictures on the walls,
Heroes, fights, and festivals;
And in a corner find the toys
Of the old Egyptian boys.

Robert Louis Stevenson

palanquin: an enclosed seat
carried on poles by servants

Why travel?

Looking at the brochure page

The brochure page on page 62 presents a particular view of travel. Look at it again and then think about these questions:

1 What kind of people is the advertisement aimed at?
2 What makes you think this?
3 Does it appeal to you?
4 What kind of travel does it offer?
5 What picture of foreign countries does it suggest?

Looking at the poem

The poem on page 63 paints many different pictures of the fantastic places the poet would like to visit.

1 Choose one that you find attractive.
2 Write out Stevenson's description.
3 Describe in your own words the picture you see in your mind as you read it.
4 Explain what you find attractive about it.

Your ideas

What fantasies do *you* have about places you would like to visit? Describe one such place: try to give a vivid picture of what you think it would be like and explain why you would like to go there.

EXT Fantasy travel agent

Now is your chance to be a travel agent offering exotic holidays in fantastic parts of the world.

Planning

Make notes as you go through these stages:

1 Choose an exciting, unusual, or fantastic travel destination.
2 Think carefully about the kind of people you want to offer your holiday to.
3 Think about the type of activities you will offer.
4 Decide what kind of accommodation will be available.

Making up an advertisement

Use your ideas to write the text for one of the following:

■ a full-page advertisement to go in a glossy magazine
■ a 30-second television commercial
■ a 30-second radio commercial.

Lost for a word?

If you are stuck for the right word to describe your holiday of a lifetime,
try some of these:

amazing	evocative	luscious	sensational
astounding	exceptional	lush	spectacular
awe-inspiring	exquisite	luxurious	strange
awesome	extraordinary	magnificent	succulent
blissful	fantastic	marvellous	sumptuous
breathtaking	glorious	memorable	unbelievable
charming	gorgeous	mind-blowing	unforgettable
de luxe	haunting	mouth-watering	unknown
delicious	idyllic	mysterious	way-out
delightful	imposing	overwhelming	wonderful
dramatic	incredible	phenomenal	
elegant	lavish	refreshing	
enjoyable	lovely	relaxing	

Meaning check

Look at the list of words in the box above. Do you know the meaning of all the words?

- If the answer to that question is 'Yes', ask a friend with a dictionary to test you!
- If the answer is 'No', make a list of those you don't know, and look them up in a dictionary.

Spelling check: words ending in -ous

Quite a few of the words in the list above end in **-ous**:

delicious	glorious	gorgeous	luscious
luxurious	marvellous	mysterious	sumptuous

1 Make sure that you can spell them.
2 Think of four more words ending in -ous.

Other endings

There are other common endings in the list. Find two more and list the words with each of those endings.

It is just unbelievable!

If you did the writing in *Fantasy travel agent* on page 64, you will probably find that you used a number of sentences like this:

It is the experience of a lifetime.
This will be the most amazing, breathtaking, mind-blowing holiday ever!

When we are describing things – real or imaginary – we use many sentences like these. They follow a similar pattern:

Subject	Verb	Rest of sentence (complement)
It	is	the experience of a lifetime.
This	will be	the most amazing, breathtaking, mind-blowing holiday ever!

These sentences use special verbs called **linking verbs**:

be/is/am/were etc
seem
appear
become

The part that follows the verb is called the **complement**, because it *completes* the meaning of the subject.

A

How would you complete these sentences by adding complements?

1 When she finally caught up with her brother, she told him he was a ....
2 The last place we lived in was ....
3 What I really dislike about supermarkets is ....
4 Whenever I see Sharon she seems ....
5 People who talk about nothing but football are usually ....

B

Think of good subjects for each of these sentences.

6 .... has become really boring recently.
7 .... are very intelligent and good-looking.
8 .... seemed very odd on Saturday afternoon.
9 .... might have been the only chance we got to win a competition.
10 .... always appears to be living in a dream.

Punctuating script

1 Look back at pages 52–56 and make sure that you can remember how to set out and punctuate a script.

2 Look at the script below. You will notice that you are not told who is speaking or what is going on. Work out for yourself who the characters are and what is happening.

3 Now write it out as a complete script, putting in characters' names and stage directions.

– Just made it!
– D'you think anyone saw us?
– Shouldn't think so.
– Hope not, anyway.
– You frightened, or something?
– 'Course not ... It's just that ...
– You are, aren't you? You're scared.
– No I'm not. Don't be stupid. It's just that ...
– What then?
– It's just that I thought I saw someone standing in the next door garden.
– When?
– Just as we were climbing over the fence.
– There couldn't have been.
– Yeah. You're probably right. That's all right then.
– What did he look like?
– Who?
– This person you saw.

Wordpower

All these words are in the unit you have been reading.

1 Explain the meaning of as many as you can.
2 For those you cannot explain, find them in the unit and try to work out their meaning from the sentence they are in.
3 For any that are left, look them up in a dictionary.
4 Make sure you can spell them all.

word	page	line	word	page	line	word	page	line
unfortunately	52	9	economic	56	160	raw-boned	60	6
immediately	52	11	litter	60	4	bay	60	6
vigorous	54	84	galaxy	60	4	swarthy	61	16
sycamore	54	92	cockatoo(s)	63	5	minaret	63	9
sobering	56	160	bazaar	63	12			
sheer	60	15	flamingo	63	21			

Cliffhangers

When you read a 'normal story', you start at the first page, and continue right through until you reach the end. But when you reach the end of a chapter in an **Adventure Gamebook** you are given a choice to make. You have to decide 'What happens next?'

The Quest for the Scroll

Chapter 15

Garth's feet were sore and his battered body ached. How far had he travelled in his quest to find the scroll that would prove his rightful inheritance? He felt dispirited and cold, wondering whether he would ever succeed. If the way back had not been as dangerous as the way ahead, he might have surrendered to his despair. With a deep sigh, he trudged on up the winding mountain path.

The day was beginning to draw in as the sun's rays lost their heat. Like a red, malevolent eye, the sun winked, and disappeared behind a jagged black peak. In the valley far below mist was already shrouding the forest being swallowed by the shadows of night. Garth felt terribly alone, wishing he was comforted by the sound of another human voice, a fire, and some food. He listened to the voices in his head which told that this was all folly, and sure to end in death.

The next moment he was face down against the stones of the mountain path with a weight on his back pressing dirt into his mouth. Arms were pinning his arms down, a knee crushed the air out of his lungs, a hand gripped the hair on the back of his head, forcing it backwards. He felt the ice cold of a blade against his throat. Realising it was useless to struggle, he willed himself to be calm, to collect his senses before acting.

The hands that held him dragged him roughly to his feet, shaking him upright. In the darkness of the mountain night he looked at his attackers. The band of brigands grinned at him with weather-beaten faces and blackened, broken teeth. Their chief sneered down at him from the horse on which he rode.

'So traveller,' he said, 'Welcome to my kingdom.'

'Not much of a kingdom,' said Garth defiantly, surveying the desolate mountainside, 'and not much of a King.'

He felt the knife-blade tighten against his throat, saw the chief's eyes narrow and flash with anger. And then the mouth hidden by his beard spread wide with laughter.

30 'Not much of a traveller,' he countered, indicating Garth's tattered cloak, his tunic torn and caked in mud. The brigands joined their laughter to their chief's, and the hand that held the knife relaxed.

'You look in need of food and shelter, traveller,' said the chief. 'Come with us to our village and we'll provide entertainment besides.'

Garth felt a hidden message pass between the brigands and their chief as grins grew wider.

'Is your food and shelter so bad, you have to issue invitations with a knife at the guest's throat?' he said. Again the chief's face darkened for a moment, but then he nodded to his men. Garth felt the knife blade nick against his 40 throat, then disappear.

He looked from one to another of the brigands. There was one way to escape, to cast himself over the edge of the path and hope that something in the dark abyss would break his fall …

Should Garth bide his time, and go with the brigands to their village?
(Go to chapter 6)
Or should he plunge to freedom into the abyss? (Go to chapter 2)

What do you think?

If you were reading this story, which of the two possibilities would you choose and why?

How gamebooks work

There are several different ways through the story. You have to make the right choices to succeed. These books are called gamebooks because they work like board-games:

1 There is a 'setting' where the game takes place.
2 There is a 'task' to complete (for example, to find out who committed a murder).
3 There are 'characters' or players, including one or more opponents to overcome.
4 There is a 'route' to follow, with obstacles to overcome and choices to make.

Storyboards

A good way of planning any story is to make a storyboard: you take a large sheet of paper and plot the different episodes of the story on it. If you like, you can draw small pictures illustrating each episode.

On pages 70 and 71 there is part of the storyboard that was used to plot *The quest for the scroll*. It does not show all the links between the episodes, but contains a lot of the story ideas.

On pages 72 and 73 is the storyboard for *Tony's troubles*, a different type of story. This shows the choices and links that are made between different parts of the story.

Look at them carefully and then turn to page 74.

The Quest for the Scroll

In the Mountains

Prince Garth is heir to the kingdom of Elsor. But proof of his claim is written in the Scroll held by the evil Scrollmaster in the Castle of Lost Causes. Garth sets out from his mountain stronghold to find the Scroll or perish in the attempt.

The Rope Bridge

Both the rope and wood are rotten. Below, rapids swirl. How can he cross?

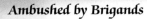

Across the Rapids

The River of Remorse foams white against rocks. Can Garth's frail craft survive the rapids?

Ambushed by Brigands

The Brigands offer to help him find the castle. Should he accept their offer of food and rest, or make a run for it?

Forest of Wolves

Close to exhaustion, Garth seeks shelter in the forest's depths. His sleep is destroyed by the nightmare howls of the demon wolves …

The Valley of Snakes

As far as the eye can see, the valley floor writhes with the deadly coils of venomous snakes. How can Garth pass through unharmed?

No traveller has ever passed through this terrible place …

Gargoyle Mountain

As he draws near, Garth senses the very rocks begin to move …

The Petrifier

One glance from the evil eyes of this hideous hag turns all who see her into stone. She may know the way into the Castle. Should Garth take the risk to learn her secret?

Skull Cave

Inside, there may
be a map.
Should he go in, or
pass by in safety?

Inside Skull Cave

The Cave is full of the
remains of those who've
entered. None escaped.
What terror lurks within?
How does Garth escape?

The Village
of Brigands

The Brigands require
payment for their
hospitality – Garth
is asked to play
cards – Death Poker!
Do the cards give him
the luck he needs?

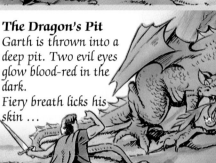

The Dragon's Pit

Garth is thrown into a
deep pit. Two evil eyes
glow blood-red in the
dark.
Fiery breath licks his
skin …

The Castle
of Lost Causes

Surrounded on all sides
by sheer cliffs, guarded
by the Undead, how can
Garth gain entry to The
Castle of Lost Causes?

The Dungeon

Captured by the Undead, what
torment and torture awaits Garth
in the Dungeon of Despair?

The Death Tower

Somewhere in the
Death Tower lurks
the flesh-eater spider.
Each step Garth takes
may break the threads
of its hideous web …

The Duel with
the Scrollmaster

The Scrollmaster sets Garth
his final task – to solve the
Riddle With No Answer.
If he succeeds, the Scroll is his.
If he fails, he must serve the
Scrollmaster for Eternity …

Tony's troubles TF

1
Tony seems to attract trouble, at home and at school. Take last night. His best mate Mark goes out with Jenny. They had arranged for Tony to go on a double date with Jenny's best friend, Sandy. Tony didn't show up. His mother left his dad last night – all hell broke out at home. His friends are mad at him, but he can't tell them the real reason. Tony is shattered. Should he bunk off from school? Or meet his friends afterwards and sort things out?

→ **9**
→ **16**

16
He meets the others after school. There's a big row about last night. Sandy gets mad and storms off. Even Mark is angry. Only Jenny tries to patch things up. If she can persuade Sandy, can Tony make the pictures tonight? Does he say he will, or that he'll think about it?

→ **3**
→ **8**

8
Jenny finally gets Sandy to give Tony one last chance. The girls are waiting outside the cinema. It's getting late, but neither of the boys has shown up. At last Mark arrives but without Tony. Jenny wants them to wait. The other two want to go without him…

→ **12**
→ **14**

14
They go on without him. Jenny is upset about it, and thinks something is wrong. Then she notices Mark is getting very friendly with Sandy. She's angry but decides to go with them to the cinema.

→ **5**

9
He decides to bunk off from school. But his tutor takes him last lesson. Maybe it would be better to hide somewhere round school, and meet the others afterwards? Or should he go down town, and maybe meet them at the cinema that night?

→ **3**
→ **15**

3
He decides to go to the cinema. He takes a short cut down by the canal. But as he jumps down from the bridge to the tow-path he slips in the mud and nearly ends up in the canal. His clothes are wet and muddy. Should he go home to get changed, or carry on into town?

→ **2**
→ **12**

12
Jenny, Mark and Sandy wait for Tony but he still doesn't turn up. Jenny is sure that there must be something wrong. She tries to get the others to go with her to call at his house. The others want to go to the cinema. There's an argument. What do they decide to do?

→ **13**
→ **5**

5
They go on to the cinema. Jenny gets suspicious when Mark sits between her and Sandy. Then half-way through the film, Tony turns up, dripping wet and muddy. There's a big row and the manager asks them to leave…

→ **7**

15 It just isn't his lucky day. He hides in the store-room in the boiler house, smoking a few fags and trying to make up his mind whether to tell the others his problem. Then the caretaker comes in. Tony gets away, but he is recognised. He goes off to his lesson, but there's a message from the Head. Should he face the music, or just go off home and leave tomorrow to look after itself?

6 The Head gives him his usual third degree. Why was he out of his lesson, did he think he could get away with it, doesn't he realise he's throwing away his chances in his exams …? Then he threatens to write a letter to Tony's parents. His dad would hit the roof! More trouble on top of Tony's mother leaving! Tony decides he had better tell the Head the whole story. To his surprise the Head is sympathetic, and says he will help in any way he can. Tony goes home feeling a bit better.

2 When he gets home he realises that he has forgotten his key. And his mother isn't there to let him in. Tony is really fed up. He could force a window and get in. And if he waits for his dad he'll be late meeting the others again. What should he do?

10 A neighbour sees someone breaking into the house next door, and calls the police. When they arrive, Tony has a hard time getting them to believe he lives there. He goes off to meet the others in a foul mood …

13 Jenny, Mark and Sandy call for Tony who has only just got into his house. He is embarrassed to see them, and makes up an excuse about his mother being out. He thinks about telling them the truth, but Mark and Sandy are being very awkward about things. Should he tell them, or just suggest going out

4 It is too late to go to the cinema, so they just wander round town. Jenny notices that Mark is paying Sandy a lot of attention. And they keep making snide remarks about Tony letting them down. He's had about enough of this …

7 Tony finally loses his temper with Mark and Sandy. In the middle of the row he tells them that his mother has left home. Mark is not very sympathetic. 'So what?' he says, 'Why didn't you just say?' Jenny loses her temper and gives both Mark and Sandy a piece of her mind …

11 Tony and Jenny go home together. They are a little surprised at the way things have turned out, and a bit shy together. Then Tony finds he can talk to her without feeling awkward. They arrange to see the film together. Perhaps his troubles are on the mend …

Writing an adventure gamebook

TF You are going to write an adventure gamebook of your own. On the next four pages there are instructions on how to prepare, plan and write it.

1 The setting and type of story

The first thing you have to decide is where and when the story is set. This will affect the type of story you write. You could choose any of the settings and types of story shown in this chart. Decide what kind of stories you like, and choose a similar setting:

Times	Places	Types
The distant past	An imaginary land	Quest / Adventure
An historical period	Another planet or world	Detective / Mystery
The present day	A real or imaginary city	Romance
The future	Your own town	Horror / Fantasy
	A foreign country	Sport / Challenge

2 The task

This provides the main idea for your story. The type of story you want to write will help you to decide on the task your heroes or heroines have to undertake. These ideas will help you choose a suitable task for your storyline.

Types	Possible tasks
Quest / Adventure	Finding an important object
	Rescuing someone
	Overcoming an enemy, discovering his (her/its) lair
Detective / Mystery	Discovering 'who done it'
	Proving yourself innocent
Romance	Overcoming a rival in love
	Proving yourself worthy
	Explaining misunderstandings
Horror / Fantasy	Escaping the clutches of someone or something
Sport / Challenge	Overcoming an opponent
	Succeeding to perform a challenge

3 The characters

It is useful to prepare files about the main characters before you begin to write, including a drawing (or possibly a picture from a magazine), so that you have a clear idea what they look like, and how they speak and act. Here's an example:

Garth

<u>Age:</u> 21

<u>Family:</u> Father was King of Elsor, poisoned by servant under the control of Scrollmaster. Mother died of a broken heart.

<u>Important events:</u> Smuggled from castle while a baby, taken to village high in the mountains. Brought up by peasant family loyal to King. On coming of age, he was informed of his rightful claim to the throne. Determined to avenge death of father.

<u>Physical description:</u> Black haired, rugged features, handsome. Deep brown eyes, determined mouth. Hands blistered from hard work, felling trees. Well-built, stocky but not tall.

<u>Clothes:</u> Coarse peasant clothes, thick cloak, well-worn boots. The only thing which shows his royalty is the magnificent sword which belonged to his father.

<u>Personality:</u> Determined, single-minded, but inclined to act first and think later. Can lose his temper easily. Loyal to friends. Brave.

<u>Friends:</u> Old Conor, the servant who smuggled him from the castle. Conor's daughter, Fia, who accompanies him (against his will) disguised as a boy.

<u>Enemies:</u> The Scrollmaster and his legion of cohorts.

Summary of what to do

1 Decide on a setting, a type of story and a task for your gamebook.
2 Write notes detailing what you have decided.
3 Decide on three or four main characters for your gamebook.
4 Prepare a character file for each one.

4 The storyline routes

In any story, the characters have to make choices when faced with problems or dangers. These choices can be planned by using a branching diagram like the one shown below, which shows how the Quest story could continue after Garth has been captured by the brigands:

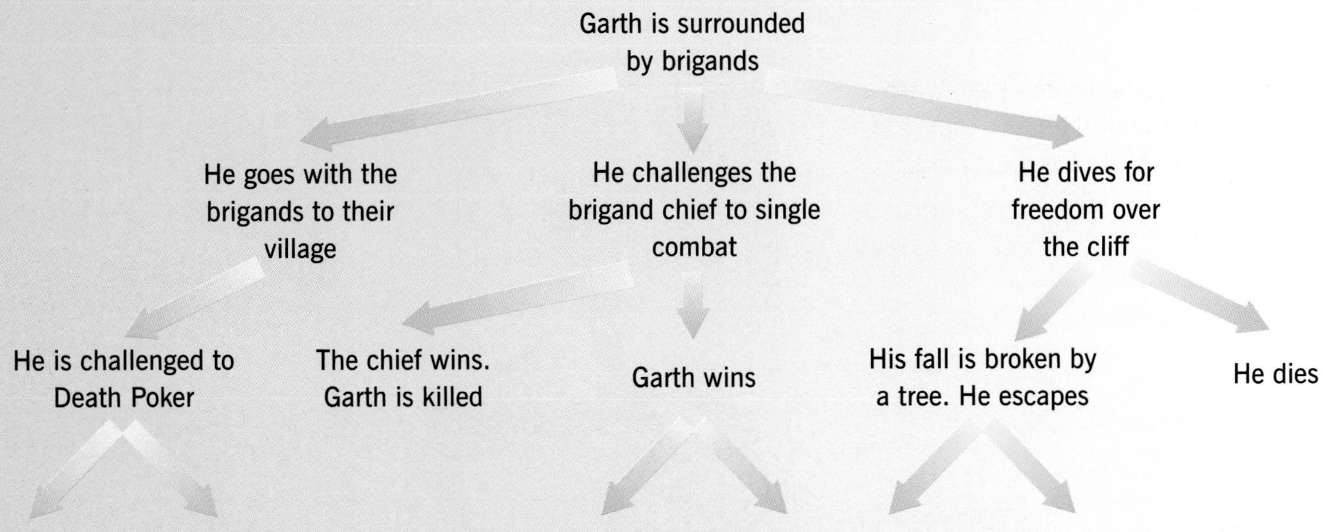

Garth is surrounded
by brigands

He goes with the
brigands to their
village

He challenges the
brigand chief to single
combat

He dives for
freedom over
the cliff

He is challenged to
Death Poker

The chief wins.
Garth is killed

Garth wins

His fall is broken by
a tree. He escapes

He dies

In a traditional story, the writer only makes use of one of these choices at each branch, using the storyline which offers most in terms of excitement and interest. The gamebook format allows a writer to develop several different storylines, and allows the reader to choose alternative routes through the story.

What to do

Make a branching plot diagram like the one above for your gamebook.

5 Planning the storyboard

You should now be ready to plan your gamebook as a storyboard.

1 Begin by dividing a large piece of paper into 16 squares. Each square will eventually become a chapter in your book:

A1	B1	C1	D1
A2	B2	C2	D2
A3	B3	C3	D3
A4	B4	C4	D4

2 In the top left-hand square (A1) write a short description of the 'task' which is to provide the main idea in your story.

3 In the bottom right-hand square (D4), explain how the story is to end, the 'showdown' when the conflict between the characters comes to a head.

4 Use your branching diagram to work out how the storylines might continue, beginning with the opening chapter. The choices given to the reader will then branch first to squares A2 and B1 and so on. Carry on filling in the board until each square contains the idea for a chapter.

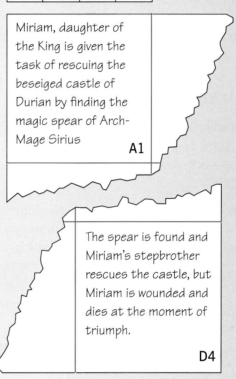

Miriam, daughter of the King is given the task of rescuing the beseiged castle of Durian by finding the magic spear of Arch-Mage Sirius **A1**

The spear is found and Miriam's stepbrother rescues the castle, but Miriam is wounded and dies at the moment of triumph. **D4**

In the mountains of despair, Miriam and the dwarf Gradrig are attacked by steel-fanged giant rats. Behind them is a dark cave. **B2**

They flee into the cave and make their way deeper into the mountain pursued by the rats. Suddenly their way is blocked by a wide river. **C2**

They decide to face the rats and fight. Gradrig draws his sword. Miriam stumbles and falls over the edge. **B3**

Hints

- It is easier to work out the storylines if you can put a separate adventure on each square.
- If things follow on from each other, make sure that this is possible.
- The more connections there are between squares, the more difficult it is to work out the storylines.

Dead ends

These are endings when you 'kill off' the character when the reader makes a wrong choice. They can follow on from any square on your storyboard. You can see examples of these on the branching diagram on page 76. But don't include too many, or your readers may give up in frustration.

6 Numbering your chapters

So far you have been working on your story in the correct order. In the book the chapters need to be in a jumbled order, so that your readers can't look ahead and work out which is the best choice to make. There are two ways of doing this:

1 Write the book as a loose-leaf. Start each chapter on a new sheet of paper. Write the story in correct order. When you have finished, re-order the chapters, keeping Chapter 1 at the beginning.
2 If you are writing the story in a book, you need to jumble the chapters before you start writing. Use your planning diagram. Give each chapter square a number. Start with 1 in the top left-hand corner, but put all the other numbers in a jumbled order, like this:

1 A1	7 B1	13 C1	9 D1
11 A2	4 B2	2 C2	15 D2
3 A3	10 B3	14 C3	16 D3
8 A4	5 B4	6 C4	12 D4

Remember:
- DO start with Chapter 1
- DON'T put the last chapter of your story at the end of the book.
- DON'T write the chapter numbers in the book.

7 Writing your gamebook

Now write your gamebook
Have fun!

Look at it from my point of view

Page	Title	What you do	Why you do it
80–81	**Look at it from my point of view**	Work in a group on seeing a situation from different points of view. Prepare a presentation and then share your ideas with the class.	To share ideas, and to practise seeing things from different points of view.
82–83	**Update**	Look at more pictures of the situation and discuss it further. Tell the whole story as if you were really there.	To get you to think about the situation as a whole. To develop your skills as a writer.
84	**Telling your story: punctuation**	Learn about the use of punctuation to mark hesitations and pauses in speech.	To improve your punctuation skills.
85–86	**First or third?**	Learn about the advantages and disadvantages of first and third person narrative. Then convert part of a story from one to the other. Revise pronouns.	To improve your story-writing skills, and develop further your understanding of how language works.
87–91	**Poor Alice**	Read the story and answer questions as you go. Look more closely at the text and use quotations to back up your ideas. Write a character sketch and write about the story from different points of view.	To develop your ability to write about literature. To learn more about viewpoint in narrative.
92–93	**Conversation piece**	Read a poem aloud with a partner. Continue the ideas of the poem in your own writing.	To improve your skills in reading aloud. To develop your imagination.
94	**Coming late**	Read a poem and think about the situation it describes. Present your ideas in the form of a table.	To broaden your ability to read with sympathy and imagination.
95	**Fiona's spelling is terrible!**	Think about spelling problems in general and your own spelling in particular. Do a survey of your own spelling.	To improve your spelling and your understanding of where and why you make mistakes.

MY POINT OF VIEW

Different people often see the same thing in different ways.
We all have an individual **viewpoint**.

Group work

Work in a group of three.
Look at the picture. Three people
have been highlighted.

1 Each choose one of the three.
2 Study the picture carefully.
3 Work out exactly what the
person you have chosen can
see.
4 Write notes describing what
you, as that person, can see.
5 When everyone is ready, take it
in turns to describe what you
can see. Speak as if you were
the person in the picture. Don't
just read out your notes – try to
make your description as lively
and personal as you can.

Making a presentation

6 When everyone has had their
turn, discuss all three. How can
each one be improved and
made more detailed and vivid?
7 Practise the descriptions again
until you are satisfied that all
three descriptions are as good
as they can be.
8 Now you are ready to present
your three viewpoints to the
rest of the class.

The Heinemann English Programme 3

Update

Do you agree?

Look at the pictures on these two pages. They show what the artist thought each of the people could see.

- Compare each one with your description.
- Has the artist seen things differently from you? If so, how?
- Who do you think is right?

The whole picture

In a situation like the one you have been describing, people do not just see things. They have other senses – and they have emotions.

- Think again about your chosen character. Imagine that you are actually there. What can you hear, taste, smell, and feel (with your sense of touch)?
- Write down everything you have thought of.
- Now think how you would feel in that situation – what your emotions would be. Describe those feelings as fully as you can.

The whole story

Now tell the whole story of what happened from your character's viewpoint.

Writing advice

This is an occasion when you should think carefully before you write. You may need to write more than one draft. **Look at pages 182–183 for more advice about this.**

Telling your story: punctuation

When people speak they often hesitate, or make sudden changes of subject. When writing speech down, use:

- three dots ... for a hesitation
- a dash – for a sudden change of subject.

And I ... er thought ... about Damon and – have you ever noticed what a big nose Mary's got?

Punctuating a transcript TF

This text is a transcript of part of an interview. Where you see this symbol: / it means that the speaker paused.

Write out the transcript, using punctuation to help make the meaning clearer. As far as possible divide it up into sentences, but do not add any words or leave any out.

Note
PA = Personal Assistant
MD = Musical Director

Example
We rang up – my my PA rang up – the ... um agents concerned and asked them to attend at a certain time in London.

Warning
If you use too many dashes it can become irritating for your readers. The dash can nearly always be replaced by another punctuation mark.

Practice
Rewrite this letter, getting rid of as many dashes as possible.

we rang up / my my PA rang up the / um agents concerned and asked them to attend at a certain time in London we always hold our auditions in London and I took with me an MD and a choreographer because / when I was looking for Peter particularly I had to be sure that the person I chose was fit enough to play the part and / because there's a lot of flying involved and / the same with Wendy and the same with the / Lost Boys and so we first of all did the professional auditions in London and whittled down to / um I think two or three / er candidates for each part until eventually we selected the those that we thought were best in some cases they were second choices because people weren't available at the end and / um sometimes we lost them to / richer companies who were able to offer them more lucrative / huh rewards but we've got ourselves a very good cast we're delighted with that

Dear Dee,

Sorry not to have written for so long – you know how it is – first the cat got run over by little Petie's trike – we had to take him to the vet – the cat I mean, not Petie – then Gran came to stay – you know how difficult she can be at times! It was all going all right until last Thursday – my usual day to go to Assertiveness and Hatha Yoga classes – they hold them at the Primary School in Phillip Street. When I told Gran I was going out she went bananas – you should have seen her face – she went on and on about how she'd come all this way to see us – which is nonsense for a start – she only lives fifteen miles away. Anyway – to cut a long story short – I'm afraid I can't come to see you next week.

First or third?

On page 83 you told the story in the first person – as an 'I story'. Many authors prefer to tell stories in the third person. Each approach has its advantages:

	I story	she/he/they story
✔	immediate and personal you get inside the character's head	you can talk **about** the characters you can see more than one person's point of view
✘	you can only describe what that person actually sees or knows about	can become rather boring and remote

You can get the best of both worlds by writing a 'she/he/they' story as if it was an 'I' story:

You write it as an I story:

I wanted to show my father that girls are as good as boys any day of the week. Better, in fact. I wanted him to notice me, not just pat me on the head and mumble and walk away. That's why I did it.

Then you go through it and change 'I' to 'he' or 'she' and 'we' to 'they':

She wanted to show her father that girls are as good as boys any day of the week. Better, in fact. She wanted him to notice her, not just pat her on the head and mumble and walk away. That's why she did it.

Now you try

1 Convert the next part of this story in the same way:

It was Thursday, the eighth of July. Our teachers were on a one-day strike so David and I were at home. At least, I was at home, feeling cross and resentful because I had been left out again. My father had taken David to show him round the laboratories. I'd wanted to go too, but they said I was too young.

When you have finished, compare the two. Which do you prefer and why?

2 Look again at the beginning of the story you wrote on page 83. Choose a section of about ten lines. Convert it into a she/he/they story in the same way. When you have done it, compare the two. Which do you prefer and why?

TF

Helpline
You may find that when you do this exercise you begin to get tangled up with the pronouns ('he', 'she' etc). If so, look at the next page which has more about pronouns.

Pronouns: reference

Personal pronouns

	Singular (one)		Plural (more than one)	
	subject	object	subject	object
1st person	I	me	we	us
2nd person	you	you	you	you
	thou*	thee*		
3rd person	she	her	they	them
	he	him		
	it	it		

Possessive pronouns

If you do change a story from the first person to the third person, you must remember to change all the pronouns. This includes **possessive** pronouns.

	Pronouns that always go with a noun *(That's her book)*	Pronouns that always stand alone *(That book is hers)*
1st	my	mine
2nd	your	yours
	thy*	thine*
3rd	her	hers
	his	his
	its	its (very rare)
1st	our	ours
2nd	your	yours
3rd	their	theirs

Note
Pronouns marked * (thee, thou, thy, thine) are nowadays only found:
- in old books
- in dialect.

Warning
Even when possessive pronouns end with the letter 's', you never use an apostrophe with them.

Poor Alice

This is a picture of the class described in the story. As you read the story, you should be able to identify some of the children. See how many you can spot.

Some people look out of the window. That way you get noticed and Sir makes you give the answer to something when you've no idea what it is because you haven't been listening. Then you get a sarky comment as well. Nathan and Wayne are even sillier. They take the ink thing out of their biros and use the plastic tube as a pea-shooter with bits of soggy paper. They always get caught but they still do it. What I do is look interested.

   I have this look. I practise it sometimes in front of the mirror. It's my 'really interested in what you're saying, Sir, and I'm doing my best

10 to follow even if I don't understand it all' face. Once I've switched it
on I can forget about the work and think my own thoughts. All the
noises in the classroom become a lovely sort of blur, but I have to
keep a bit of my brain tuned in, in case he calls my name. I'm the
only Fiona in the class so that makes it easier. There are four Kellys. I
don't know how they cope. Sometimes I quite like my name. Other
times I hate it but I suppose most people are like that. People with
unusual names want ordinary ones and all the Johns and Janes want
to be called Conan or Christobelle. When we're supposed to be doing
written work I usually write any old rubbish in my rough book, but
20 every now and then I look up with a serious-thinking expression till
Sir notices me.

'Fiona.'

'Yes, Sir.'

'Would you go downstairs to the staffroom and ask whoever's
there for some merit slips?'

'Yes, Sir.'

'How are you getting on with your work?'

'Fine, Sir.'

I wonder if he believes me or if he thinks it's easier to pretend. He
30 doesn't much like my exercise book. Sometimes when he does his
marking in the lesson I've watched him. He always starts with Alice
Tonks' book. She's clever and her work's always tidy. He leans back
in his chair and smiles. Every now and then he writes something on
the page. It can't be spelling mistakes because Alice is a walking

dictionary. It's probably a little comment like 'Brilliant' or 'I wish I'd thought of that'. Alice knows when he's marking her book too and she does her best to throw him one of her flirty smiles. When he comes to my book he looks at the cover for a moment, his face goes all panicky as if he's just been dumped in the ring with a Sumo wrestler, then he shuffles the book to the bottom of the pile.

'Quick as you can, Fiona.'

'Yes, Sir. Sorry, Sir. Just finishing a sentence.'

Five minutes later and I'm back. He looks a bit pained and glances at his watch, but at least I don't have to explain why I spent half a minute getting down there and four and a half on the way back because I slipped into the toilets just to waste a bit of time.

He takes the merit slips and starts filling them out. We're supposed to be doing an exercise on speech marks. Sir spent twenty minutes talking about them. I lost track after the first example and switched off, so now I'm just writing down the words and dropping these huge 66's and 99's over a few of them. He hates us calling them 66 and 99. 'You should have grown out of that by now,' he says. 'A 99 is an ice cream, not a piece of punctuation.' I make sure I laugh with the others.

Sometimes I feel like I'm sliding down a very slippery pole and I don't know what's at the bottom, but it's very dark down there and when I land I'll probably hurt myself. Then I think well school isn't everything. People get on all right even if they haven't got a load of GCSEs. Mind you, if you're a girl it helps if you're pretty, and no one could ever accuse me of being pretty. My nose is too big, my chin's too small and my spots won't go away. Of course, Alice has perfect skin as well as brains. Mrs Phillips, our RE teacher, told us about Job and how God made him suffer all sorts of horrible things, to test him. One thing he got was a plague of boils. We had to draw Job in our books and I drew him getting the plague of boils, only it wasn't Job, it was Alice. Mrs Phillips didn't notice the difference, even though my Job had a cute little turned-up nose and an expensive perm.

Sir's filling in the merit slips now and Alice is looking smug. I can't quite believe it, but I got one once. For English! I nearly died of shock. He called me up and I had to sit next to him while he went over this work I'd done. It was a piece from a diary. He read it out as he marked it, quite quiet but I could see some of the others trying to listen. He kept putting in bits of punctuation and changing spellings so fast I couldn't keep up with him. Then he wrote: 'This has its problems, Fiona, but you really make the reader feel what's going on. MERIT.' He said if I wrote it out again correctly he'd like to put it on the wall, or even in the school magazine. I wouldn't, though. Alice and her friends would only sneer at me and say, 'Sir wrote that, not

Questions

1 Who is telling this story?
2 What have we learned about her so far?
3 Who is Alice and what is she like?
4 How do you think the story will develop?

you.' And anyway it's too personal. Sometimes when I look at it
80 I feel pleased I got the merit and sometimes I just feel sad. It wasn't an easy thing to write.

Febuary 17 on a Saterday morning my littel sister Sara dide and I was there. She had ben ill about a mounth it was her brain the Dokter said. I rembered the day I was playing whith her she was drest up in my t shirt much to big for her like a long dress and she got her feet all tangeld up. She didnt hert herself tho she sort of sat on her bum on the floor and smiled then we had tea and she wasnt well her head hert and she cride. After she was very sick but we didnt no how bad she was. When mum took her to the Dokter I was scard for her but Mum said itll be allright
90 but I new she was rong. I cant explan how but I new.

There are another two pages, the most I ever wrote. Alice read her diary entry to the class. It was about her getting a pony and how she goes down to the stables every evening to see him and brush him, and how sad she is when it rains and she can't go.
'Wayne!'
'Yes, Sir?'
'Give me that.'
'What, Sir?'
100 'Don't "What Sir" me. You know very well.'
'It wasn't me. It was him, Sir.'
'Nathan, is that true?'
'No, Sir.'
They're both hiding their pea-shooters under the desk, on their knees and trying to look innocent. They couldn't look innocent if you paid them.
'Right, I'm not wasting any more time on this now. You can come back at lunchtime and we'll sort it out then.'
'But, Sir.'
110 'Lunchtime!'
Alice has this big smile on her face. 'Sir, shall I give out the merit slips for you?'
Sir smiles back. 'Sorry, Alice. They're not for you today. They're for my next class.'
Poor Alice.
Sometimes life's hard.

Rex Harley: *Poor Alice*

Questions

5 What were your thoughts and feelings when you read Fiona's diary?
6 Why did her teacher give her a merit mark for it?
7 What do you think of what Alice wrote in her diary – compared with Fiona's writing?
8 Why does the story end with those last two sentences?

What's she like ... and who says so?

Divide a piece of paper into two columns. In the left-hand column write one or two sentences in answer to each of these questions:

1 What kind of person do you think Alice is?
2 Do you think Fiona's description of her is fair?
3 What are your impressions of Fiona as a person?
4 What do you think Alice's opinion of Fiona might be?

Making notes

Now look back at what you have written. For each sentence find the part of the story which gave you that idea. Write down the page and the line number(s) in the right hand column opposite the sentence.

Writing a character sketch

Use the writing you have done so far to write a paragraph each about:

■ Alice
■ Fiona.

Each paragraph should contain:

■ sentences stating what you think of the character
■ explanations of why you think that.

Further writing

These writing topics are more difficult and need more thought. You will find it helpful to make notes (as you did above) before you start writing.

Through Alice's eyes
The story shows us Alice through Fiona's eyes. Imagine that you are Alice. Write a description of Fiona as you see her. Use as many of the factual details from the story as you can – including the occasion when Fiona was awarded a merit mark for English.

What 'Sir' thinks
How do you think the teacher sees Fiona and Alice? Imagine he has to write their English reports. He is in the staff room thinking about what to say and he talks to another teacher about the girls. Write the conversation they have and end by telling the reader what he writes in their reports.

Conversation piece

Late again Blenkinsop?
What's the excuse this time?
Not my fault sir.
Who's fault is it then?
Grandma's sir.
Grandma's. What did she do?
She died sir.
Died?
She's seriously dead all right sir.
10   That makes four grandmothers this term.
And all on PE days Blenkinsop.
I know. It's very upsetting sir.
How many grandmothers have you got Blenkinsop?
Grandmothers sir? None sir.
None?
All dead sir.
And what about yesterday Blenkinsop?
What about yesterday sir?
You missed maths.
20   That was the dentist sir.
The dentist died?
No sir. My teeth sir.

You missed the test Blenkinsop.
I'd been looking forward to it too sir.
Right, line up for PE
Can't sir.
No such word as can't. Why can't you?
No kit sir.
Where is it?
30   Home sir.
What's it doing at home?
Not ironed sir.
Couldn't you iron it?
Can't do it sir.
Why not?
My hand sir.
Who usually does it?
Grandma sir.
Why couldn't she do it?
40   Dead sir.

Gareth Owen

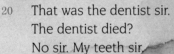

Pair reading

This poem is written like a play script. Practise reading it aloud with a partner. In your reading:

- try to develop voices for the teacher and Blenkinsop
- think about how the teacher's mood might change as the conversation progresses
- think about the pace of your reading – how does it vary as the poem proceeds?

Excuses, excuses!

1   Make a list of excuses for:

- things that you should have done, but have not
- things you have done that you should not have done.

Think about home, as well as school, and include realistic excuses as well as improbable and even crazy ones.

2   Now use your list to write 'Conversation Piece 2': use the poem as a pattern for a second conversation between Blenkinsop and 'Sir'.

Time to spare?

Why not write 'The beginner's handbook of excuses' – with guidance on the right excuse for the right occasion?

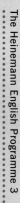

Coming late

Isabel comes late to school.
Tight as a bud in winter
into herself she curls
when our teacher reprimands her.

You are a slack and lazy girl.
You won't be any good …
(The voice has risen to a howl
of wind above a frozen wood)

… until you learn to come on time
10 and take more pride and show you care.
Isabel hides a living pain
beneath her blank and frosted stare.

She cannot say her dad has gone,
her mum is ill, she has to dress
and feed her brothers, copes alone
without complaint; will not confess

her courage in a shrivelled life,
will not admit to anyone
that deep inside her is a fragile leaf
20 craving some warmth to open into sun.

Barrie Wade

Thinking about the poem

1 Why is Isabel late for school?
2 How does her teacher react?
3 What are your thoughts and feelings
   about the teacher, and why?
4 What are your thoughts and feelings about Isabel,
   and why?

Facts and feelings

5 Read the poem again and make some notes about it,
   using a diagram like the one on the right.
6 Look at the notes you have made. In what ways can
   you add to your answers to questions **3** and **4**?

Facts	Teacher's feelings	Isabel's feelings
Isabel is late again	angry	

Fiona's spelling is terrible!

That's what a lot of people might say if they read her diary on page 90.
But her teacher gave her a merit mark.

1 If you had been her teacher would you have done the same?
2 How important is spelling: what effect does the bad spelling have on
   you when you read the diary?
3 Is spelling equally important in everything you write, or does it
   depend?
4 If the answer to question 3 is 'it depends', what does it depend on?
5 Do different people have different attitudes to spelling? For example,
   think about:

- your friends
- your English teacher
- other teachers who teach you
- parents or other adults you know.

Different kinds of spelling mistake

One of the most important things to understand about spelling is that
there are several different ways in which you can get a spelling wrong.
Understanding what kind of spelling mistake you have made is half way to
avoiding that mistake again. Look at Fiona's diary again and use a copy of
the chart below to put her spelling mistakes into types. Some of them will
appear in more than one column. In the last column write the correct
spelling.

spelling	letters swapped round	writing it as you say it	missing out a letter	adding a letter	using the wrong word	other	correct spelling
Febuary		✔	✔				

How about you?

Now think about your own spelling. Read through some of the writing you
have done recently and find the spelling mistakes in it. Use a copy of the
chart above to find out which types of spelling mistake you make most
often.

TF

See you soon?

Page	Title	What you do	Why you do it
97	**See you soon?**	Read the facts about blindness. Then start to think about it in more depth. Try thinking which of your five senses is most important to you.	To start you thinking about the themes of the unit.
98–99	**Close your eyes**	Think about the hazards for visually handicapped people in ordinary situations. Experience through drama what it is like to be visually handicapped. Imagine a day as though you were blind.	To imagine yourself in someone else's position. To get you to share your ideas.
100–102	**Silent Wednesday**	Read an extract from a novel and give your first impressions of it. Look at the text in more detail and find all the evidence that you used in your answers. Think again about your original answers, and add or change anything you need to. Write a continuation to the story.	To develop your reading skills. To make you think carefully about your answers, and to improve your writing skills.
103–105	**Loving without seeing**	Read a transcript of a radio broadcast and give your first reactions to what you have read. Write an article using the material provided. Look through the transcript again and find examples of the differences between speech and writing.	To improve your skills as a reader and a writer; to develop your understanding of how language works.
106	**This really clean smell of 'Bold'**	Continue your work on the differences between speech and writing, by looking at how the speakers used adverbs.	To develop your understanding of language by learning about adverbs.
107–108	**Blinking hell**	Look at an advert and think about the effect it has on you and the ways in which that effect is achieved; make up your own advert for a local radio programme.	To study how advertising media work.
109–111	**Making fun**	Read an extract from a Shakespeare play, and think about the situation and characters it presents. Think about how compound words are formed and used.	To develop your skills as a reader and to learn more about Shakespeare. To increase your understanding of English words.
112	**Punctuation Wordpower**	Practise punctuation and spelling and do a wordpower exercise.	To practise punctuation and spelling and to develop your vocabulary.

See you soon?

FACT

The official definition of blindness is when a person cannot see how many fingers are being held up at a distance of 10 feet.

FACT

Only 8 in every 100 blind people were born that way. The rest become blind as the result of an illness or an accident.

FACT

Guide Dogs for the Blind train 1,000 dogs every year. Most of the dogs are golden retrievers or labradors.

FACT

Out of approximately one million blind and partially sighted people in Britain, nearly three quarters of a million are female.

Starting to think

1 You have five senses: hearing, sight, smell, taste, touch. How important is each of these? Put them in order of their importance to you.

2 Think about these activities. Which senses do you need for each one?

- riding a bike
- reading a book
- doing pottery
- fishing
- going for a walk
- gardening.

3 This unit is about sight … or the lack of it. Which would be more difficult: to be born blind or to lose your sight? What are your reasons for your opinion?

The Heinemann English Programme 3

Close your eyes

Blind to the hazards

Many blind or partially sighted people complain that society is blind to the hazards it creates.

- What potential problems can you see in the street scene on these pages?
- What could be done to help with any of these problems?
- Which are the three most serious problems and why?

And in school?

What problems can you see for a blind person:

- in your classroom
- in your school as a whole?

What could be done to cut down the number of problems?

Drama

Work in pairs

One of you is the blind person; the other is the guide.

1 The guide must lead the blind person round the room by the touch of a fingertip and clear but quiet instructions.
2 When you have done this, change roles so that you have both played the part of the blind person.
3 Talk about:

 ■ how it felt to rely on someone else
 ■ how it felt to be responsible for the blind person.

What about me?

Imagine that at some moment in a normal day you found that your sight was fading almost to nothing. Think about these questions:

 ■ What happens?
 ■ What does it feel like?
 ■ How do you cope?

Now tell the story of that day.

Silent Wednesday

The Day of the Triffids by John Wyndham tells the story of William Masen. It starts in a hospital where he is covered in bandages after an eye operation. Waking on Wednesday morning, the hospital seems strange and silent. Eventually he takes off his own bandages to see if he can find out what is going on …

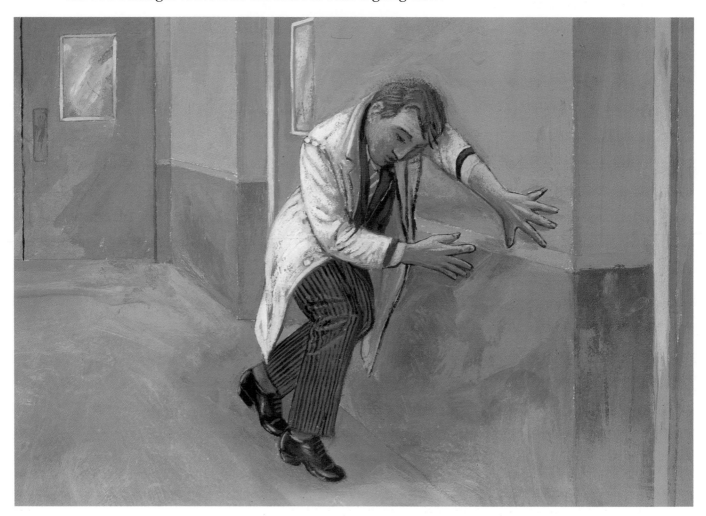

When I first looked along the corridor I thought it empty, then as I moved forward I saw a figure come out of a shadow. He was a man wearing a black jacket and striped trousers, with a white cotton coat over them. I judged him to be one of the staff doctors – but it was curious that he should be crouching against the wall and feeling his way along.

'Hullo, there,' I said.

He stopped suddenly. The face he turned towards me was grey and frightened.

See you soon?

'Who are you?' he asked, uncertainly.

'My name's Masen,' I told him. 'William Masen. I'm a patient – Room 48. And I've come to find out why –'

'You can see?' he interrupted, swiftly.

'Certainly I can. Just as well as ever,' I assured him. 'It's a wonderful job. Nobody came to unbandage my eyes, so I did it myself. I don't think there's any harm done. I took –'

But he interrupted again.

'Please take me to my office. I must telephone at once.'

I was slow to catch on, but everything ever since I woke that morning had been bewildering.

'Where's that?' I asked.

'Fifth floor, west wing. The name's on the door – Doctor Soames.'

'All right,' I agreed, in some surprise. 'Where are we now?'

The man rocked his head from side to side, his face tense and exasperated.

'How the hell should I know?' he said, bitterly. 'You've got eyes, damn it. Use them. Can't you see I'm blind?'

There was nothing to show that he was blind. His eyes were wide open, and apparently looking straight at me.

'Wait here a minute,' I said. I looked round. I found a large '5' painted on the wall opposite the lift gate. I went back and told him.

'Good. Take my arm,' he directed. 'You turn right as you come out of the lift. Then take the first passage on the left, and it's the third door.'

I followed instructions. We met no one at all on the way. Inside the room I led him up to the desk, and handed him the telephone. He listened for some moments. Then he groped about until he found the rest, and rattled the bar impatiently. Slowly his expression changed. The irritability and the harassed lines faded away. He looked simply tired – very tired. He put the receiver down on the desk. For some seconds he stood silently, looking as though he was staring at the wall opposite. Then he turned.

'It's useless – dead. You *are* still here?' he added.

'Yes,' I told him.

His fingers felt along the edge of the desk. 'Which way am I facing? Where's the damned window?' he demanded, with a return of irritability.

'It's right behind you,' I said.

He turned, and stepped towards it, both hands extended. He felt the sill and the sides carefully, and stepped back a pace. Before I had realised what he was doing he had launched himself full at it, and crashed through …

John Wyndham: *The Day of the Triffids*

1 Thinking about the story

■ Why do you think the doctor jumps from his window?
■ What do you think might have happened to cause these strange events in the hospital?
■ If most people were blind and only a few people could see, how might that change the kind of world we have?

2 First impressions

This passage is the first and last appearance of Doctor Soames in the novel. In a short space, John Wyndham gives us plenty of information to enable us build up an impression of him. Write the answers to these questions:

1 What do you think he looks like?
2 How does he speak?
3 How does he behave towards William Masen?
4 What is your overall impression of him?

3 Looking at the details

When we read a story we **interpret the evidence** that the writer presents. Most of the time we do this without thinking about it, but from time to time it is useful to take a closer look at how we do it. Look at the answers you wrote for *First impressions*. For each one:

1 Look back at the passage and find *all* the evidence that relates to that question.
2 Write down the line numbers of the sentences that contain it.
3 Think again about your original answers.
4 Add anything that you have missed out and change anything that you now think is incorrect.

4 Continuing the story

What might happen to William Masen next?

1 Where might he go?
2 Whom might he meet?
3 What would his thoughts and feelings be?

Write the story of the rest of that Wednesday.

Writing advice

For more advice about answering questions that test your understanding, look at pages 180–182.

Loving without seeing

The BBC Radio 4 programme *In touch* asked a number of visually handicapped people: 'If you are blind or partially sighted how can you tell you're in love? How important is vision when it comes to finding a mate, or perhaps just a date?' These are some of the responses.

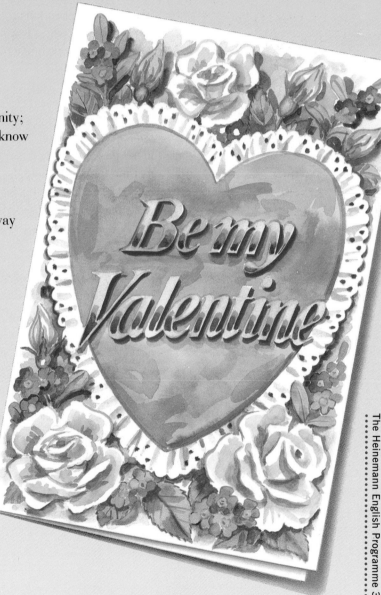

Speaker 1
What attracts me to a man is usually his quiet masculinity; it's usually somebody who is very sort of strong – you know – puts his arms around you firmly but doesn't actually bully you when he's doing it.

Speaker 2
There is something about movement, and touch, the way one touches you ... gentle. It is very important that I should touch them, and know if they are slim or fat.

Speaker 3
My hands must go to his face first, not because I care how he looks, but to feel whether his face has got the same kind of humanity I can hear in the voice. So the first thing I go for is laughter lines. If there are laughter lines around his eyes he's in with a pretty strong chance. Then if he's got curly hair and I can snake my fingers around the back of his neck and tangle my fingers in his hair he's definitely in with a chance... The last thing, I think, is he's got to have a nice neat little bum!

Speaker 1

When I first met my current partner we used both to be in a big gang of people that went to pub quizzes. The first thing that attracted me to him was his voice; he had a very nice voice. I liked his voice, and something about him: he was very laid back, you know, very centred. He wasn't bothered about impressing people or showing off or anything like that. But he was the one that answered most of the questions correctly, so I liked that. And when I used to sit next to him sometimes, he did smell very nice.

Speaker 4

30 When I was visiting Wales a few years ago, I took my guide dog for a run along the beach and at the end of this beach there was some rocks to get up on to the promenade. And somebody was obviously very concerned for my well-being, and [that] I wouldn't go falling over these rocks, [and] came to help me. It was quite a breezy day and whilst helping me across the rocks – whilst I was holding on to this person's arm – her hair, which was fairly long, got caught in a breeze and blew in my face. And I think it was that that won me. I'm not with that person anymore, but I'll always remember the hair, and the shampoo, the smell.

Speaker 5

Bold 3 does it for me. When it comes to *Bold 3* soap powder, I have to say it really,
40 in my past, has turned me on. Don't ask me why, but it has done the trick. When I met my future husband, he came into the room – and I'd never really met him before – and he had this jacket on, which was bobbly and rather old, but had this really clean smell of *Bold* about it. And every time I saw him it was the smell that sort of reminded me it was him, really.

Speaker 4

If somebody can sing as well as speak nicely, then I'm going to go for it. I think my ideal love would be a piano player, somebody who can sing as well – could have midnight duets around the joanna, with the perfume and the hair and the aura.

Speaker 6

50 There was a survey not long ago. I think it was in Canada – it may have been in the United States – which showed that marriages where one partner is blind have fewer divorces than almost any other category of married people. And may I say that my wife and I celebrated our Golden Wedding last year, and we still send each other Valentines!

First reactions

What were your first reactions to the answers?

1 Did anything you read surprise you? If so, what and why?
2 Did anything you read amuse you? What and why?
3 A common reaction to the thought of being blind or partially sighted is that you must *lose* so much. What do you think these speakers have *gained*?

Questions

Imagine you had the opportunity to question one of these speakers.
1 Which one would it be and why?
2 Make a list of at least four more questions you would like to ask that person.
3 Now do the same for a second speaker.

Writing

Using the transcript, write an article for a magazine. The editor has told you that you should write 150–200 words and include some direct quotations from the transcript.

1 Decide which magazine you are going to write for.
2 Think carefully about the readership of that magazine. What kind of writing do they like? Decide on the 'line' you are going to take.
3 Make up a title that communicates this idea.
4 Make a list of the key points that you think your article should contain.
5 List the quotations you want to use.
6 Write the article.

Speech and writing

The text you have been reading is a **transcript**. This means that it contains all the words that were spoken. In order to make it easier to read, punctuation marks have been added and 'ums' and 'ers' have been removed. Even so it is easy to see that it is **speech** written down.

1 Read through the transcript again.
2 Find three or four parts which make it clear that this is **spoken** English.
3 Write them down.
4 For each one explain what makes it clear that the words have been spoken.

This really clean smell of 'Bold'

Look again at this extract from the transcripts on pages 103–104:

When it comes to Bold 3 soap powder, I have to say it really, in my past, has turned me on. Don't ask me why, but it has done the trick. When I met my future husband, he came into the room – and I'd never really met him before – and he had this jacket on, which was bobbly and rather old, but had this really clean smell of Bold about it. And every time I saw him it was the smell that sort of reminded me it was him, really.

Various things tell us that it is spoken English: one of them is the repetition of 'really'. Just count how many times she uses it!

What is it for?

Try reading the extract out loud missing out 'really' each time it occurs.

1 What difference does it make?
2 Why does the speaker use the word?
3 Look back at the transcript. Can you find any other words that are used in a similar way?

What does it *really* mean?

Words like 'really' and 'obviously' are **adverbs**. They have a wide range of meanings and uses.

Use
Adverbs work with verbs, adjectives and other adverbs.

Meaning
Adverbs answer questions like these:

Where? *She went **away**.*
When? *I met him **yesterday**.*
How? *They were chatting **happily** when I left them.*
How much? *Mary is **deeply** unhappy.*

TF

Adverbs, please

Complete these sentences by adding suitable adverbs.

1 Jo did _____ in the Maths test.
2 The smell of farmyards makes me feel _____ sick.
3 After school I'm going _____.
4 I told you: I finished that book _____.

> ## Writing advice
> Look for opportunities to use adverbs effectively in your own writing.

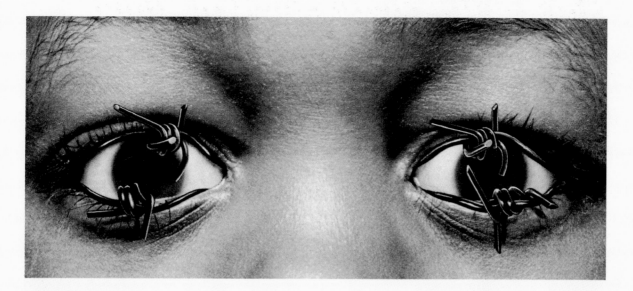

Blinking Hell

At first it's not too bad.

And it's easy to see how it's spread. Just watch a child for five minutes. They don't sit still for a moment. They're always poking their fingers into something they shouldn't, then rubbing their eyes with grubby fingers.

And that's all it takes to spread trachoma.

You only notice there's something wrong when the child's eye starts to itch and swell up. It's not terribly nice but it's bearable, and the infection will "burn" itself out after a few weeks, leaving just a small scar on the eyelid.

The trouble is, it'll be back. And it won't just come back once. It will strike over and over again, with every re-infection burning and scarring the child's eyelids a little bit more.

In the end, after years of suffering, the eyelids become so scarred and disfigured that the eyelashes turn inwards, into the eye.

Imagine, every time you blink, you scratch your eyes.

Until, agonisingly slowly, you go blind.

Think about it ... you've probably blinked a dozen times since you started reading this. What if you'd scratched your eyes every time? You'd be in agony and you'd be doing everything you could to stop. But how do you stop blinking?

You may never even have heard of trachoma before, but six million people in the developing world are blind because of it. And millions more are carrying the infection. It makes life impossible for young mothers trying to raise children. Fathers and husbands can't work to support themselves, let alone their families. So the whole family suffers.

And the utterly horrifying thing is, their suffering is totally unnecessary, because trachoma can be treated very quickly and cheaply in its early stages with ointment.

The ointment is called Tetracycline and it costs as little as £1.20 to treat one person. But this is still too much for many people in the developing world, which is why we're asking you to help.

With £12 you can help relieve the suffering of 10 young people with trachoma. £60 will help relieve the suffering of 50 more.

You can even help with the more advanced cases, which can be treated with an operation to turn back the ingrowing eyelashes, so they stop scratching the eye. This sight saving operation costs just £5. So a donation of £25 will pay for five operations by a paramedical worker, and £50 will help save the sight - and relieve the suffering - of 10 more people.

Wouldn't you pay a hundred or a thousand times that if it were your eyes at stake? Please help by sending a donation with the coupon to:

Sight Savers, FREEPOST,
Haywards Heath, W. Sussex, RH16 3ZA

Or you can call our credit card hotline
(Visa/Access) on 0444 412424.

Reg. Charity No. 207544

YES, I want to help save someone's sight

My gift is ☐ £12 ☐ £25 ☐ £50 ☐ £60

☐ £100 ☐ £250 ☐ Other £ _____

Please make your cheque payable to Sight Savers, or if you wish to pay by Access or Visa enter your cardholder no. in the boxes below.

TM30

Card expiry date _____

Cardholder's Signature _____

Mr/Mrs/Miss/Ms _____ Initials _____
(BLOCK CAPITALS PLEASE)

Address _____

_____

_____ Postcode _____

Please return this coupon with your donation to:
Sight Savers, FREEPOST, Haywards Heath, West Sussex RH16 3ZA

Sight Savers International is not a large charity so it does not have a massive advertising budget. The advertisements it produces are especially important in getting the message and appeal across. Look carefully at the one called 'Blinking Hell'. Think about what you learn and how you feel about the situation that the advertisement describes.

The picture

1 What was your reaction when you first saw the picture on the advertisement?
2 Why does the picture have this effect on you?
3 The advertisers could have chosen a close-up photograph of someone suffering from trachoma. How would this have changed the effect of the advertisement?

The title

4 What do people normally mean when they say, 'Blinking hell'?
5 What do the words mean here?
6 How does this contribute to the total effect of the advert?

The facts

7 What is trachoma?
8 How do people catch trachoma?
9 What effect does trachoma have?
10 If you catch trachoma many times, what starts to happen?
11 What is the final result of getting trachoma again and again?

The message

12 In what order does the advertisement present its ideas?
13 What does it do to bring the message home to the reader?
14 Why do you think the advertisement goes into detail about the costs of treating trachoma?
15 What do you think is the most effective feature of this advertisement?

Sight Savers on local radio

You have been given a 40-second advertising slot on local radio to tell people about Sight Savers and trachoma. The advertisement has two purposes:

■ fund raising
■ letting people know about the charity's work.

Plan and produce this radio slot. You will need about 120 words. As you are fund raising, you will need to give a telephone number and/or address for donations.

TF

Making fun

People who are blind or partially sighted are not always treated with sympathy. In this extract from *The Merchant of Venice* by Shakespeare, we see an old blind man being tricked by his son. Read the text and then look at the activities on page 111.

Launcelot Gobbo is employed by a Jewish merchant called Shylock. He has decided that he wants to leave and find work elsewhere. Almost immediately he meets his father in the street.

GOBBO	Master young man, you I pray you, which is the way to master Jew's?
LAUNCELOT	[*Aside*] O heavens, this is my true-begotten father, who being more than sand-blind, high-gravel blind, knows me not – I will try confusions with him.
GOBBO	Master young gentleman, I pray you which is the way to master Jew's?
LAUNCELOT	Turn up on your right hand at the next turning, but at the next turning of all on your left; marry at the very next turning turn of no hand, but turn down indirectly to the Jew's house.
GOBBO	Can you tell me whether one Launcelot that dwells with him, dwell with him or no?
LAUNCELOT	Talk you of young Master Launcelot? [*Aside*] Mark me now, now will I raise the waters. Talk you of young Master Launcelot?
GOBBO	No master sir, but a poor man's son. His father, though I say it, is an honest exceeding poor man, and God be thanked, well to live.

sand-blind: partially sighted
Mark: pay attention to
raise the waters: call up a storm

The Heinemann English Programme 3

LAUNCELOT	Talk not of Master Launcelot father; for the young gentleman – according to Fates and Destinies and such odd sayings – is indeed deceased, or, as you would say in plain terms, gone to heaven.
GOBBO	Marry God forbid, the boy was the very staff of my age, my very prop.
LAUNCELOT	Do I look like a cudgel, or a hovel-post, a staff, or a prop? Do you know me father?
GOBBO	Alack the day, I know you not young gentleman, but I pray you tell me, is my boy – God rest his soul – alive or dead?
LAUNCELOT	Do you not know me father?
GOBBO	Alack sir I am sand-blind, I know you not.
LAUNCELOT	Nay indeed, if you had your eyes, you might fail of the knowing me: it is a wise father that knows his own child.
GOBBO	Pray you sir stand up, I am sure you are not Launcelot, my boy.
LAUNCELOT	Pray you, let's have no more fooling about it, but give me your blessing. I am Launcelot your boy that was, your son that is, your child that shall be.
GOBBO	I cannot think you are my son.
LAUNCELOT	I know not what I shall think of that; but I am Launcelot the Jew's man, and I am sure Margery your wife is my mother.
GOBBO	Her name is Margery indeed. I'll be sworn if thou be Launcelot, thou art mine own flesh and blood.

Lord worshipped might he be, what a beard hast thou got; thou hast got more hair on thy chin than Dobbin my fill-horse has on his tail.

prop/...cudgel, or a hovel-post, a staff, or a prop: Gobbo calls his son a 'prop' – meaning support. Launcelot thinks he is calling him a 'stick'.
man: servant
fill-horse: horse used to pull a large wagon

Funny?

When Shakespeare wrote this scene it was intended as a piece of knockabout humour between two clowns.

1 Do you think that a modern audience would be likely to find it amusing?
2 Is there anything about it that a modern audience might object to?
3 Can you think of television comedy shows that contain sections that people object to? If so, what do they dislike?
4 How do you think this scene should be tackled in a modern production?

Fathers and sons (and mothers and daughters)

1 Launcelot says, 'It is a wise father that knows his own child.' Can you think of modern situations that illustrate how parents may not know their own children? Describe one such situation.
2 Choose one of these two short sections to work on:

- line 6 ('Turn up on…') to line 8 ('…the Jew's house.')
- line 15 ('Talk not of…') to line 17 ('…gone to heaven.')

Imagine that this situation is being presented in a modern play. Think about the language that Launcelot might use. Write a modern version of that speech.

Sand-blind

The adjective *sand-blind* probably comes from an old word **sam**blind. The first three letters mean 'half' – as in *sam-dead* and *sam-ripe*. Launcelot thinks it has got something to do with having sand in your eyes and so makes the comment about his father being 'gravel-blind' – which is presumably even worse than sand-blind.

semi-
The modern prefix that means half is *semi-*.

1 How many different words can you think of that begin with this prefix?
2 Write them all down.
3 Write down the meaning of each.
4 Now explain what you think each of these words means:

semi-annual	semi-basement	semi-precious
semi-nocturnal	semi-professional	semi-liquid
semi-submersible	semi-cylinder	semi-rigid

5 If a semi-quaver in music is a note that is half the length of a quaver, what do you suppose a hemi-demi-semi-quaver is?

Punctuation

This is how the story on pages 100–101 continues. Try to work out what it is saying. Then write it out using all the necessary punctuation.

i didnt look to see after all it was the fifth floor when i moved it was to sit down heavily in the chair i took a cigarette from a box on the desk and lit it shakily i sat here for some minutes while i steadied up and let the sick feeling subside after a while it did i left the room and went back to the place where i had first found him i still wasnt feeling too good when i got there at the far end of the wide corridor were the doors of a ward the panels were frosted save for ovals of clear glass at face level i reckoned there ought to be someone on duty there that i could report to about the doctor i opened the door it was pretty dark in there the curtains had evidently been drawn after the previous nights display was over and they were still drawn sister i enquired she aint ere a mans voice said

Spelling

-ie- or -ei-?
Copy out these words and fill in the gap correctly:
th–f   rec–ve   w–rd   rec–pt
fr–nd   s–ze   gr–f   conc–t

-ar, -er, -or?
Copy out these words and fill in the gap correctly:
burgl–   doct–   calend–   design–
inspect–   read–   vineg–   sail–

Wordpower

All these words are in the unit you have been reading.

1 Explain the meaning of as many as you can.
2 For those you cannot explain, find them in the unit and try to work out their meaning from the sentence they are in.
3 For any that are left, look them up in a dictionary.
4 Make sure you can spell them all.

word	page	line	word	page	line	word	page	line
interrupted	101	12	bewildering	101	19	exasperated	101	24
apparently	101	28	receiver	101	38	irritability	101	37
impatiently	101	36	agonsingly	107	23	disfigured	107	19
infection	107	33	developing	107	32	unnecessary	107	39
suffering	107	46	horrifying	107	38	paramedical	107	54
advanced	107	49	ointment	107	41			

The Jerry Holdsworth File

LOCAL BOY'S LUCKY ESCAPE

The next six pages follow the same story through the eyes of some of the people involved. As you go through each stage of the story you should follow these steps:

1 Work out what has happened.
2 Look at the character who is telling that part of the story. (This is shown in the frame labelled *Storyteller*.)
3 Think about how that character would have understood what happened and what they would have thought and felt.
4 Write the story as that character would tell it. The *Storyteller* frame gives you a starting point.

Storyteller

Storyteller

The whole story

With the pictures on this page you can use your imagination to work out what happened to Jerry and how he was rescued.

Jerry's story

1 Study the pictures above carefully, and tie them in with the pictures on the preceding pages.
2 Make a list of the main events throughout the whole story, in the correct order.
3 Go through the list. Against each event put one of the marks from the list on the right.
4 Think about what Jerry would have thought and felt at each stage of the story.
5 Think about who he might have told his story to – and how he would have expressed himself to that person.
6 Now write Jerry's story.

How to mark your list

✔ If Jerry knew about it first hand.
? If he didn't know about it first hand, but would probably have been told about it by someone else.
✗ If he probably would not have known about it.

Local paper

A reporter from the local newspaper interviewed all the people who knew anything about Jerry and what happened to him. She pieced together all the information and then wrote a complete story under the headline on page 113. Use your list of what happened and write the local paper report.

Going bananas

Page	Title	What you do	Why you do it
122–123	**Going bananas**	Talk about words that have been borrowed from other languages, what they mean and how they are used.	To introduce the theme of the unit: words and where they come from.
124–127	**Song of the banana man**	Read a poem and answer the questions. Think about your answers and then write a paragraph describing the central character in the poem. Focus on the language used in the poem.	To read a poem with enjoyment and understanding. To develop your reading and writing skills.
128	**English in India**	Read about the British in India. Do reserach into words which have come into English from Indian languages.	To learn more about where different words come from.
129–133	**Life in an Indian village**	Read an extract from an autobiography and think about how it is constructed. Study it in detail and write a summary of information selected from it.	To develop your reading and writing skills.
134–136	**On the bank of the River Birupa**	Study how the writer constructs a paragraph. Look at the use of adverbial phrases.	To develop your skills as a writer, and to learn more about language.
136	**Wordpower**	Do a wordpower exercise.	To develop your vocabulary.

banana (b«'na:n«). Also 7 bonana, bonano.
... ...nana (the fruit), banano (the tree), given by De Orta

GOING BANANAS

Pacific; it grows ...
purple spot...
2. a. Th... ...lusters of angular, finger-like
... ...ous and highly nutritious
...ip.
b. The yellow colou... ...a (=F. banane).
3. pl. Crazy, mad, wild (w... ...tration, etc.), esp...
in phr. to go (also drive) bana... skin (also fig...
4. attrib., as in banana-leaf, -tree (... ...nthornus
(sense 2); banana bird, a gregarious ... ...lied to
icterus), belonging to the Starling fami... ...d in the
certain South American and West Indian ...
genus Icterus; also = banana quit;
banana boat, a boat carrying bananas; also ...
1945);
banana flour, a...
banana fly (see...
banana liquid (...
banana-oil,
(a) = banana ... ...haviour;...
(b) slang, nons...
sauce;
banana quit: s... ...sp. in central
banana repub... ...dent on its fruit-

...ca, who... exporting trade;
banana solution, a solution, having the odour of bananas, used as

What do you know about bananas?

1 When did you last eat a banana?
2 What country did it come from?
3 How do you know?
4 Where does the word 'banana' come from?
5 How do you know?
6 How many different expressions can you think of that contain the word 'banana'?

This unit

In this unit we look at words and where they come from and the ways in which English has been influenced by some of the different countries in which it is spoken.

Words ... from all directions

English has been borrowing words from other languages for hundreds of years. Some came through colonisation, but others arrived through trade, travel and international exchange.

Country of origin

Below are a number of words and some information about them. Study the material below carefully and then draw up a table like the one on the right.

Word	Meaning	Country of origin
dock	a place where boats can tie up and be unloaded	Holland

Words

admiral	canoe	cola	chocolate
journey	paper	piano	typhoon

Information

- When Columbus reached the Caribbean he found the local inhabitants used an open boat, which in the language of Haiti was called a canoe.
- In West Africa there is a tree called the Cola tree, which produces edible nuts. These are used in the manufacture of several popular soft drinks.
- In Ancient Egypt a writing material was made from a reed which the Greeks called παπυροσ, or papyrus.
- Centuries ago in Mexico a food was made from the seeds of two trees, the cacao and the pochotl. They called it chocolatl.
- The Arabic for 'chief' is amir. The word al, meaning 'the' comes after the noun, so 'the chief of the water' is amir-al-ma.
- In Italian the words for 'soft and loud' are 'piano e forte' – which is how a well-known musical instrument got its name.
- The Old French word 'journée' mean's a day's work or travel.
- In Chinese 'tai fung' means 'a big wind'. In Urdu 'tufan' means a violent storm.

So *how*?

How do you think these words came to be part of the English language?

Song of the banana man

Tourist, white man wiping his face,
Met me in Golden Grove market place.
He looked at my old clothes brown with stain
And soaked right through with the Portland rain.
He cast his eye, and turned up his nose
And said, 'You're a beggar man I suppose,'
He said, 'Boy get some occupation,
Be of some value to your nation.'

I said, 'By God and this big right hand
10 You must recognise a banana man.'

Portland: an area of north-eastern Jamaica

Up in the hills where the streams are cool,
Where mullet and janga swim in the pool,
I have ten acres of mountain side
And a dainty foot donkey that I ride
Four Gros Michel and four Lacatan
Some coconut trees and some hills of yam
And I pasture on that very same land
Five she goats and a big black ram.

That, by God and this big right hand
20 Is the property of the banana man.

I leave my yard early morning time
And set my foot to the mountain climb
I bend my back for the hot-sun toil
And my cutlass rings on the stony soil,
Clearing and weeding, digging and planting,
Till Massa sun drop back a John Crow mountain
Then home again in cool evening time
Perhaps whistling this little rhyme,

Praise God and this big right hand
30 I will live and die a banana man.

Banana day is my special day
I cut my stems and I'm on the way
Load up the donkey, leave the land
Head down the hill to banana stand,
When the truck comes down I take a ride
All the way down to the harbour side;
That is the night when you tourist man
Would change your place with a banana man.

Yes, praise God and my big right hand
40 I will live and die a banana man.

mullet: a fish
janga: prawns
Gros Michel and **Lacatan:** types of banana
cutlass: long bladed knife used by farmers

The bay is calm and the moon is bright
The hills look black though the sky is light
Down at the dock is an English ship
Resting after her ocean trip
While on the pier is a monstrous hustle
Tally men, carriers all in a bustle
With the stems on their heads in a long black snake
Some singing the songs that banana men make.

Like praise God and my big right hand
50 I will live and die a banana man.

Then the payment comes and we have some fun
Me, Zekiel, Breda and Duppy Son
Down at the bar near United wharf,
Knock back a white rum, bus' a laugh
Fill the empty bag for further toil
With saltfish, breadfruit and coconut oil
Then head back home to my yard to sleep
A proper sleep that is long and deep.

Yes, praise God and my big right hand
60 I will live and die a banana man.

So when you see these old clothes brown with stain
And soaked clean through with Portland rain
Don't cast your eyes nor turn your nose
Don't judge a man by his patchy clothes
I'm a strong man a proud man and I'm free
Part of these mountains part of this sea
I know myself and I know my ways
And will say with pride to the end of my days,

Praise God and my big right hand
70 I will live and die a banana man.

Evan Jones

Reading

1 As you read the poem could you 'hear' the voice of the man who is speaking? (If not, read it again to yourself and try to imagine him speaking.)
2 How would you describe the way he speaks to us?
3 Choose a section of ten lines and practise reading it aloud so that it sounds as you think it should.

Responding

4 Look again at the first section. What impression do you get of the tourist and why?
5 How does the banana man earn his living?
6 How does he feel about his life?
7 The tourist says that he should 'be of some value to' his 'nation'. Do you think he is, or not? What are your reasons?
8 The banana man says that on banana day the tourist would change places with him. Why do you think he says that? Is he right?

Writing

9 Think back over your responses to the questions and the work you did on reading the poem aloud. Write a paragraph describing the banana man:

- his way of life
- his thoughts and feelings
- your impression of him as a person.

Language

10 The banana man is a Jamaican. In what ways does his language differ from Standard English? Think about:

- vocabulary – does he use any special words?
- grammar – does he construct sentences in a special way?
- accent – is there anything in the poem to suggest how he pronounces English?

English in India

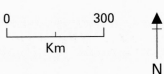

0   300
Km
N

The British first went to India to trade. In the seventeenth century the East India Company became wealthy and powerful, with fortified bases in Bengal, Madras and Bombay. Gradually the company expanded its power until it came to govern large areas of India. The British Government slowly took over that power until by the middle of the nineteenth century India became part of the British Empire. With the expansion of British power went the wider use of English. Even after Independence, English remained a major language in India. Because of the large number of local languages used in India, Pakistan and Bangladesh, English is still widely used as people's second language.

Indian in English

Large numbers of British civil servants, soldiers, and traders went to India and lived there for many years. As a result many words from Indian languages came into English. For example, the city of Calicut (modern day Kozhikode) on the Malabar coast was famous for its cotton cloth. This was called 'calicut' which later became calico.

What do they mean? Where do they come from? [TF]

thug	curry	coolie	guru
jungle	jute	chintz	cheroot

Use the information below to help you complete the table on the right. You may find that you need to use a dictionary as well.

Word	Meaning	Origin
thug	a brutal violent ruffian or	Hindi word for

Hindi wordlist

thag	*cheat, swindler*
jangal	*desert, waste, forest*
guru	*teacher, priest*
chint	*something with different coloured patches*

Tamil wordlist

kari	*sauce or relish eaten with rice*
shuruttu	*a roll (for example of tobacco)*
kuli	*hire, hired man*

Bengali wordlist

jhuto	*a braid of hair*

Calicut (Kozhikode)

Key

Urdu

Hindi

Punjabi

Bengali

Tamil

Life in an Indian village

Despite the huge influence the British had on some aspects of Indian life, much of the heart of India remained unchanged. Prafulla Mohanti was born in north-east India in the first half of the twentieth century. He studied in Bombay and then worked as an architect in London in the 1960s. After that he became a painter and writer. Here he describes his early life in a country village south-west of Calcutta.

I am the youngest son of a Karan family from the village of Nanpur. It is situated on the bank of the River Birupa in the Cuttack district of Orissa. The river gives Nanpur its identity. It provides a meeting place for the villagers, who use it for bathing, washing, and cleaning the cattle. The children love to swim in its clear blue water. In the monsoon the river overflows and the crops are often ruined. The whole area turns into a lake and the villages look like islands. In the summer the river dries up and provides a clean bed of silver sand for the children to play on.

A

My village has a population of about three thousand living in six settlements separated by mango groves and paddy fields. Each settlement is mainly inhabited by one particular caste. Caste is the most important feature in the village. It defines a person's place and the work he is expected to do. Traditionally there are four castes — Brahmins, the priests; Kshatriyas, the warriors; Vaishyas, the businessmen; and Sudtas, the servant class. The Brahmins belong to the highest caste and only they can perform the

B

ceremonies required by Hindu religion. Over the years there have been many sub-castes relating to professions. Apart from the Brahmins there are Karans — the administrators, farmers, carpenters, astrologers, potters, jewellers, washermen; and Harijans — formerly called Untouchables. The Brahmins,

20 Karans, and the Kshatriyas belong to the higher castes and are not expected to do manual work. The villagers are mainly farmers and craftsmen. Each craft is the property of a particular caste and provides a specialised family trade. Together they form the village community.

The villagers are Hindus. They believe in God, karma (fate), and the cycle of rebirth. For them God is everywhere — in a man, in a tree, in a stone.

Every village has a local deity. In Nanpur it is a piece of stone decorated with vermilion paste. It is called Mahlia Buddha. He sits under the ancient varuna tree protecting the village. The story goes that he was donated to the village by the barber's great-great-great-grandmother many generations ago.

30 Since then the barber's family has the exclusive right to attend to the deity. Mahlia Buddha had a special power to cure smallpox and cholera, and people from the surrounding villages came to worship him. Although modern medicines have now brought the epidemics under control, the power of the deity has not diminished. People believe in him and worship him for everything, even for modern medicines to be effective. Clay animals are presented. It is believed that Mahlia Buddha rides them during the night and goes from place to place guarding the village.

Every villager has a jatak, which is a birth certificate inscribed on a palm leaf by the

40 village astrologer. He is consulted for everything, whether the planets are favourable and the auspicious times for starting a journey. There is a saying, 'Tuesday night and Wednesday morning, wherever you go you receive good luck.'

The villagers live in joint families. Parents and sons live together with their families and share food cooked in a common kitchen. The houses are built of mud walls and thatched

50 roofs with outside and inside verandahs. A central private courtyard provides shelter from the sun and is mainly used by the women. Every house has an altar containing the tulashi plant (sacred basil). This herb is so valuable for its medicinal properties that it is worshipped as a goddess. The joint family system ensures that everybody is looked after. Because there is a great respect for old age the old people are never neglected.

C

D

E

Marriages are arranged by parents, and the bride and bridegroom must belong to the same caste. The girl's father has to give a dowry, and the bride must be a virgin. Widows are not allowed to remarry. They lead very austere lives. When their husbands die they break their glass bangles and stop wearing the vermilion spot on their forehead.

The role of a woman in my village is that of a mother. She has the responsibility of managing the household. If she does it well, she is compared to Lakshmi, the Goddess of Wealth, but if she destroys its unity she is compared with Kali, the Goddess of Destruction. Her duty is not complete until she has produced a son, essential for the family to continue. A house is not a home without a child.

The women in Nanpur worship Satyapir, a Hindu-Muslim god, to bless them with sons. 'Satya' is the Hindu part, meaning 'truth', and 'Pir' in Islam means 'prophet'. There is a large Muslim settlement two miles from Nanpur, and in a village on the other side of the river, a single Muslim family lives among Brahmins. The worship of a Hindu-Muslim god was a deliberate attempt to bring the two communities together through religion. In spite of Hindu-Muslim tensions in other parts of India, the atmosphere around the village has remained tranquil.

My eldest brother died in childhood. Several years passed and my mother did not have a son. She worshipped Satyapir every day. My brother was born. He was named Fakir Charan, the Feet of the Fakir, the Muslim holy man.

Religious fasts and festivals play a great part in the life of the village. The most popular is the spring festival of Holi, when the villagers throw coloured powder and water on each other as an expression of love. It represents Krishna's love play with the Gopis (milk maidens). As the cuckoo sings, hidden among the mango blossoms, welcoming the spring, the villagers carry Gopinath (Krishna) in a palanquin around the village, singing and dancing to the sound of cymbals, drums, and flutes.

All-night plays and concerts take place in the open air. Snake charmers, puppeteers, and wandering singers visit during the dry season. A wave of excitement goes through the children when they approach the village. There is no television but some villagers have radios; listening to film music is popular.

Time is measured by the sun. The day begins with sunrise, around six, and ends with sunset, twelve hours later. The pace of life is slow and nobody is in a hurry. Days become weeks, weeks turn into months, and months into years. Age has no specific meaning, and time and life continue after death. The saying, 'Time is money', has no significance in the village. There is plenty of time to gossip or do nothing and there is no boredom. The villagers discuss their personal problems with each other, sharing joys and sorrows. Life revolves around the children and the gods. Parents have no other interest.

My childhood was happy. We lived in a joint family. My father worked as a forester away from home and I was looked after by my mother, grandmother and many uncles and aunts. In my great-grandfather's time there were about twenty in the family: my great-grandfather, his wife, their two sons, and their wives and children. They lived in six rooms and ate from a common kitchen. They all contributed to the running of the house and the children were treated equally.

Prafulla Mohanti: *Through brown eyes*

I

J

Seeing the pattern   TF

1   The passage is divided into ten sections, each of which has a
    letter. If you had to give each section a title, these would be
    suitable for the first five:

    Religion – Geography – Family life – Caste – Astrology

    As you can see, they are not in the right order. Can you match
    each title to the correct section?
2   What would be good titles for sections F to J?

Looking at the detail

For each question that follows:

- find the section that deals with it
- read it carefully
- explain in your own words what the writer has to say about
  the topic.

1   How do people in the villages entertain themselves?
2   How important are women in the village society the writer is
    describing?

Summing up

1   Think about what the writer has to say about Holi.
2   Find the section of the passage that is about the topic.
3   Read it again, carefully.
4   Make notes on it, like those opposite.
5   Close the book and then use your notes to write a short
    paragraph, of not more than 50 words, about the topic.
6   Read that section of the passage again to make sure that you
    have not missed out anything of importance.
7   Now repeat the activity for one of the topics in the list below.

Holi

Springtime festival

Villagers throw coloured powder
and water

Topics

- Relationships between Hindus and Muslims
- Caste
- Families and home life.

On the bank of the River Birupa

In this description of life in India the writer paints a vivid picture of his village and its inhabitants. Each paragraph follows a clear pattern. For example, the first paragraph tells us:

why the writer is interested in this particular part of India

what gives the area its character and shape

I am the youngest son of a Karan family from the village of Nanpur. It is situated on the bank of the River Birupa in the Cuttack district of Orissa.

The river gives Nanpur its identity. It provides a meeting place for the villagers, who use it for bathing, washing, and cleaning the cattle. The children love to swim in its clear blue water. In the monsoon the river overflows and the crops are often ruined. The whole area turns into a lake and the villages look like islands. In the summer the river dries up and provides a clean bed of silver sand for the children to play on.

where the village is

how the seasons affect the people's lives

TF ## Writing for an outsider

Prafulla Mohanti writes so well that although you have probably never been to India – and certainly could not have seen it at the time he is describing – he creates a vivid picture in our minds. Imagine that you have been given the same job, but in reverse: to write a paragraph describing your locality for someone from India who has never left the country area where she or he lives.

1 Think about what your reader will need most help in picturing.
2 Think about the pattern that Prafulla Mohanti uses and create a similar one.
3 Jot down the main points you need to make.
4 Write a paragraph of between 75 and 150 words describing your locality.

Building sentences $\boxed{\text{TF}}$

If you look at the way the sentences in the paragraph are built up, you will see that they contain a number of phrases that answer the question: **Where?**

> *It is situated **on the bank of the River Birupa.***

1 How many more phrases can you find in the paragraph that answer the question 'Where?'

When?

2 There are two phrases in the paragraph that answer this question. Can you find them?

And these?
There are other phrases like this:

> *It provides a meeting place **for the villagers.***

3 Find two more phrases like this.
4 What kind of information do they give us?

Adverbials

All the phrases you have been looking at are called **adverbials**. They form an essential part of some sentences and answer questions like 'Where?', 'When?', 'How?', 'How much?', and 'Why?'

Subject	Verb	Adverbial
It	is situated	on the bank of the River Birupa in the Cuttack district of Orissa

1 Look at the paragraph you wrote for *Writing for an outsider*. See if you have used any adverbials.
2 If you have, write them down.
3 For each one, say what kind of information it gives the reader. (For example, does it give information about *Where?* or *When?*)

Using adverbials

1 For each of these adverbials:

- write a sentence that uses it correctly
- explain what type of information it gives the reader
  (which of the questions on the right does it answer?).

Where?
When?
How much?
Why?

underneath a large sports car
for years and years
after a lot of hesitations
for them to eat after school

2 Write a paragraph of not more than 100 words using as
many of these adverbials as you can:

without even looking in my direction
beside a large and very ugly traffic warden
after a silence of several seconds
in an attempt to attract my attention
at over seventy miles an hour

Wordpower

All these words are in the unit you have been reading.

1 Explain the meanings of as many as you can.
2 For those you cannot explain, find them in the unit and
try to work out their meaning from the sentence they
are in. Then check them in a dictionary.
3 If there are any left, look them up in the dictionary.
4 Make sure that you can spell them.

word	page	line	word	page	line	word	page	line
monsoon	129	5	identity	129	3	deity	130	26
settlements	129	10	caste	129	11	vermilion	130	27
donate(d)	130	28	epidemic(s)	130	33	auspicious	130	42
inscribe(d)	130	39	unity	131	67	basil	130	54
verandah(s)	130	50	atmosphere	131	77	sacred	130	54
contribut(ed)	132	108	specific	132	97	palanquin	131	87

The letter plot

Page	Title	What you do	Why you do it
138–139	**The letter plot**	Look at pictures introducing a scene from *Twelfth Night* by Shakespeare. Talk about the situation and characters they show. Write about your first impressions of the characters.	To start you thinking about the scene that forms the main part of the unit. To begin to imagine yourself into the situation.
140–146	**Finding the letter/Reading the letter**	Read the scene with help from pictures and explanations.	To develop your skills as a reader.
147	**Drama group work**	Use different drama techniques to imagine yourself into the situation, and put yourself into the shoes of some of the characters.	To develop a fuller understanding of Shakespeare's text.
148	**What happens next?**	Think about what happens next. Think more fully about the central character and write about him in a modern setting.	To continue exploring the text imaginatively and to deepen your understanding of it.
149	**Shakespeare's language**	Look more closely at the ways in which Shakespeare uses language.	To broaden your understanding of the language.
150–152	**Word invaders**	Learn about the history of English.	To broaden your understanding of the language.
153	**A slice of nice**	Look at over-used words in English.	To broaden your understanding of the language.

THE LETTER PLOT

What's going on?

This picture shows a scene from a stage production of a play. The people you can see at the back are hiding in a 'tree'.

- What do you think is happening?
- Why are the people at the back hiding?
- Who is the person in front?
- What is he reading?

What kind of people?

Look closely at the photographs. What kind of people do you think they show?

Filling in some details

Each of these photographs shows a character from a play. Suppose they were people you met in ordinary life:

- What kind of jobs might they do?
- What might other people think of them – and say about them?
- How do you think they would behave, move, and speak?

Writing them up

1 Choose one of the photographs and make up a 'character file' for that person – write out the answers to the questions, with any other details you can make up about them.
3 Now do the same for a second character.
3 Imagine a modern situation in which the two people might meet and have a conversation.
4 Write their conversation:

- as a story, using direct speech
- as a script.

The characters

The picture on the first page of this unit shows a scene from *Twelfth Night* by Shakespeare. There are five main characters involved in this part of the play:

Olivia
A wealthy young woman, alone in the world since the death of her brother whom she loved very much.

Sir Toby Belch
Olivia's uncle who sponges off her. Spends all his time eating, drinking and making merry.

Malvolio
Olivia's steward – he is in charge of running her house and estate – a very responsible job.

Sir Andrew Aguecheek
A rich and foolish young man. He has more money than sense. Toby sponges off him, too.

Maria
A member of Olivia's staff. Her job is to accompany Olivia and look after her needs.

The situation

Malvolio has criticised the behaviour of Toby, Andrew and Maria after an all-night party at which they kept everyone awake. They decide to get their revenge by making up a letter and hiding it in the garden where he is sure to find it. Toby, Andrew and Fabian, a friend, will hide themselves so that they can see what happens when he finds the letter.

Finding the letter

Explanations

she did affect me: that Olivia had a soft spot for me
one of my complexion: someone of my appearance
overweening: arrogant

sitting in my state: Malvolio imagines himself sitting on some kind of throne, with his 'courtiers' all round him

The Heinemann English Programme 3

Explanations

branched velvet gown: a long garment of velvet with a leaf design embroidered on it

kinsman: now that he is (in his dream) married to Olivia, he is related to Toby, her uncle

courtesies: bows

amend: get rid of

hand: handwriting

in contempt of question: without question

liver and all: the liver was believed to be to home of people's emotions, so this means 'emotions and everything'

Questions

1 What do we learn about Malvolio's thoughts and feelings in the picture 1 on page 141?

2 What does Toby think of this?

3 Malvolio has a fantasy about what life could be like. What is it?

4 What do we learn from it about his attitude to Sir Toby?

5 Why does Malvolio think the letter is from Olivia?

Reading the letter

Remember who commended thy yellow stockings, and wished to see thee ever cross-gartered. I say, remember. Go to thou art made, if thou desirest to be so. If not, let me see thee a steward still, the fellow of servants, and not worthy to touch Fortune's fingers. Farewell. She that would alter services with thee.

The Fortunate Unhappy

15

This is open …every reason excites to this, that my lady loves me. She did commend my yellow stockings of late, she did praise my leg being cross-gartered; and in this she manifests herself to my love. I thank my stars I am happy… Here is yet a postscript.

Thou canst not choose but know who I am. If thou entertainest my love let it appear in thy smiling; thy smiles become thee well. Therefore in my presence still smile, dear my sweet, I prithee.

The Heinemann English Programme 3

Explanations

M, O, A, I doth sway my life: the letters MOAI (all in Malvolio, but not in the right order) govern her whole life

fustian: a heavy cheap cloth – so the riddle is heavy but not worth anything

In my stars I am above thee: her luck (star sign) has made her his social superior

commended: praised

thou art made: you've got it made

steward: a servant responsible for running the whole household

fellow: equal

would alter services: would like to change places

excites: leads

manifests herself to my love: makes it clear that she loves me

Thou canst not choose but know: you must know

If thou entertainst my love: if you accept my love

become thee well: are very suitable for you; make you look even better

Questions

6 What further clues does Malvolio get to convince him that:

- the letter is from Olivia
- it is intended for him?

7 What does the letter tell him that he must do if he wishes to win Olivia's love?

Explanations

when the image of it leaves him he must run mad: when he realises the truth he will go mad

the fruits of this sport: the results of this trick

abhors: cannot stand

Drama group work

The characters

The pictures of the characters give you a good idea of what they might look like. Shakespeare gives other clues in the text – even his choice of names like Belch!

To get the most fun out of this situation actors have to use these clues to create larger than life characters. Actors have to decide how to play the following:

- movements – does the character shuffle or leap about the stage? Does s/he move very slowly or quickly?
- gesture – does the character repeat any particular gestures? Are these gestures funny?
- posture – how does the character stand? Does he/she walk upright or in a hunched position?
- voice – does the character speak with any particular accent? Is the voice hard or soft? Is the tone gentle, harsh, kind or mocking?

For example, Aguecheek could be portrayed as a tall, spindly man with angular, awkward movements, as if he was a big, clumsy puppet, with a squeaky voice or a very deep voice.

In groups, experiment with a variety of exaggerated characterisations – using a short section of the text. Try out your interpretation on the rest of the class.

Painting a portrait

A 'drama' portrait means using one person in the group to represent a painting of a character, while the others become the artists deciding how the character should look. As the others suggest new ideas, the 'portrait' has to move, following their instructions. This is a useful activity because it makes you argue about the character and his personality traits, using the evidence of the text.

Olivia has employed a portrait artist to do a selection of court portraits.

In groups create sets of portraits of the four plotters and their victim. Each of you should represent one of the characters. Develop your ideas to show:

- the artist's sketches. These capture an essential element of the characters' personalities. They may show just a part of the subject, for example Maria's face with a certain look.
- the finished portraits. These are less than flattering.

  You could then show these to another group. This might provoke an outraged response from the character's representative in that group – who could then try to persuade the artist to make more flattering alterations.
- dream portraits. Imagine the characters bribe the artist to produce their dream portraits! What would these be like?

What happens next?

This picture shows what happens when Malvolio next meets Olivia.

1 What do you think each of them is saying?
2 Describe what happens, either as a story or as a script.

A modern-day Malvolio

What impressions have you formed of Malvolio as a person?

1 Make a list of all the adjectives you can think of to describe him.
2 Can you think of any good things to say about him?
3 What do you think he would be like at each of these jobs:

- school caretaker or janitor
- traffic warden
- Managing Director of a large company
- supermarket checkout operator.

4 Choose a modern job for Malvolio and write a description of how he behaves when he meets and works with other people.

Fall guy

The trick that Maria plays on Malvolio could be played again today. For example:

> Film studio car park supervisor – everyone hates him because he's so bossy and self-important. One of the cameramen finds out that he has a crush on a famous starlet. He and a friend make up a letter which pretends to be from her to the car park supervisor, saying how much she loves him.

Write the story of what happens when the 'fall guy' finds the letter. You can use the situation described above, or you can make up one of your own. If you use your own situation, you will need to explain the background to the reader.

Shakespeare's language

The situation in the scene from *Twelfth Night* is not particularly complicated, but you may well have found the language difficult at times. There are three reasons why this might be so:

TF

- Shakespeare had a huge vocabulary and used words that you may not know.
- Words have changed their meanings since he was writing.
- He was very inventive in the way he used language.

1 Shakespeare's vocabulary

The words in the table below all come from the scene. They are all still in use but they can be replaced by a simpler word. Find the words and complete the table.

Word	Simpler version
overweening	
	bows
employment	
sway	
commend	

2 How the language has changed

Twelfth Night was probably written in 1601. Since then English has changed in two ways:

1 Words have 'died', or changed their meanings and new words have been introduced into the language.
   Examples:
   fustian: no longer used
   hand: meant handwriting then, but is not normally used to mean that now
2 The grammar of the language has changed.
   Examples:
   'Tis: now we would say *It's*
   Thus makes she: now we would say *This is the way she makes*

Find other examples of these two kinds of change and explain what the words and phrases would be in modern English.

3 Shakespeare's inventiveness

Shakespeare loved playing with words.

1 At one point in the scene, Andrew cries out from his hiding place:
   'Pistol him, pistol him' (picture 3).
   - What does this mean?
   - Find other examples of where the characters cry out from their hiding places and explain what their expressions mean.

2 Shakespeare gives Malvolio a pompous and elaborate way of speaking. Look at his speeches in picture 1 on page 141 and in picture 15 on page 145, for example. How would you express these more simply?

Word invaders

One of the reasons why Shakespeare was able to use such a wide vocabulary is that the English language contains a huge store of words. Whilst most people use about 5000 words in the course of their everyday life, the *Oxford English Dictionary* offers a choice of over half a million. If you add in scientific, technical and old-fashioned words, you can increase that number to around two million.

English has been a great collector of words over the centuries. The English language has been like a river into which different streams have flowed as time has gone by. Here are just a few examples of the words that have joined over the years.

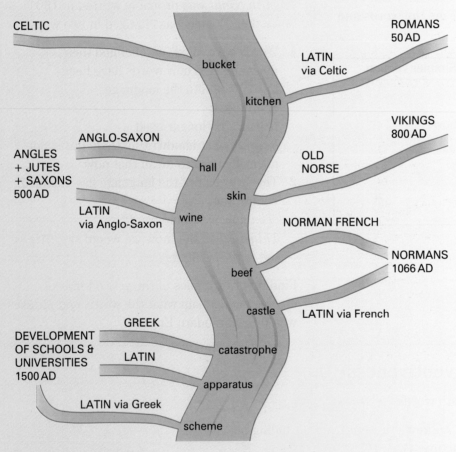

Thinking point

- What new words and expressions can you think of that have come into English in the past 50 years?
- Where do you think they came from?

TF

Roots and branches

The original word that gives rise to a group of words in a language is called a **root**. This is a good name, because when you start exploring how a word has developed, you often find a number of **branches**. The earliest language which contributed words to English is Latin.

Originally Latin was spoken by the Romans who brought it to Britain nearly two thousand years ago. Invasion is not the best way to make friends and very few Latin words remained when the Romans left.

Latin had more influence in other parts of Europe which the Romans controlled, however, and Britain acquired many Latin words indirectly. The biggest collection of these came from France as a result of the Norman Conquest.

The end of the invasions was not the end of Latin influence. The church used Latin almost all the time and so did the universities. As late as 1750, many British scholars, teachers and scientists were as fluent in Latin as in English.

The words that we have borrowed over the centuries from Latin are many and varied. Here is one example:

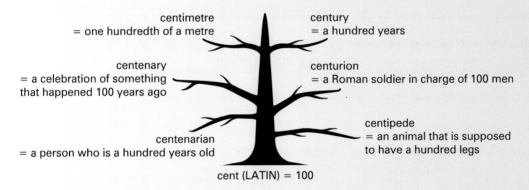

centimetre
= one hundredth of a metre

century
= a hundred years

centenary
= a celebration of something
that happened 100 years ago

centurion
= a Roman soldier in charge of 100 men

centipede
= an animal that is supposed
to have a hundred legs

centenarian
= a person who is a hundred years old

cent (LATIN) = 100

You try

Make your own versions of the following two trees, adding as many branches as you need.

porto = I carry

aqua = water

TF

Old English

The Angles, the Jutes and Saxons settled in Britain at roughly the same time. The language they spoke was generally similar and was the foundation of **Old English** or **Anglo-Saxon**. If you are looking for a straightforward word, there is a good chance that you will choose something from Old English: words like *folk, hill, fat.*

The influence of Old English can also be found in the names of towns and cities.

Old English word	Its meaning	How the word changed
tún	town	ton
hám	home	ham
leah	wood	ley
worp	enclosure	worth
feld	open country	field
ingas	the people	ing

Knowing this, Buckingham can be traced back as the home of Bucca's people. What local place names can you recognise as coming originally from Old English?

TF Double value

At its height, the Roman Empire covered most of Europe. As a result, Latin crops up all over the place. When the Angles, the Jutes and Saxons settled in Britain, they brought not only their own words, but words they had borrowed from Latin as well. The words had changed when they were absorbed from Latin and many of them changed again when they arrived in Britain. How do you think this table should be completed?

Latin	Old English	Modern English
caseus	cese	cheese
vinum	win	
flasca	flasce	
strata	strat	
vallum	weall	

A slice of nice

Nice is a word with a long and interesting history. Look at the diagram to see how it has changed over the centuries.

Starting out as the kind of word you might use as a term of abuse, it eventually became a compliment. Today it is one of those words that has been used so often it seems to mean almost anything, or nothing.

Meanings, please

What do you think the word means in these sentences?

- It was a very nice meal.
- We had a nice babysitting arrangement until the accident.
- He was just a nice person.
- You cannot get a nice piece of fresh fish these days.
- You seem to have got yourself into a nice mess.

Over-used words

Nice and other words such as pretty share the problem of being over-used. They can nearly always be replaced by another word or phrase which would fit just as well and which would be more descriptive.

1 Make a collection of words and phrases that you believe are used too often.
2 When you have a good collection, write a short conversation between two neighbours using as many of them as possible. You could use one of these settings:

- hanging out the washing
- mowing the lawn
- mending the car
- cleaning the windows.

  Don't forget to give nice and pretty a good airing along with all the others.

Nice

Today	?
	pleasant
	well-mannered
	careful
	selective
	meticulous
	over-fussy
	hard to please
The Middle Ages	stupid

Nice

A story about a toygum

This project is about making up stories for young children. It takes you through the stages of research, planning, writing and publication. It is based on the writing of a class of 13-year-olds in Avon, who wrote stories for children in a local primary school.

Discuss

1 Can you remember the stories you used to read or have read to you when you were very young?
2 What do you remember about the characters and what they did?
3 Can you remember any of the pictures in the books?
4 Were there any stories that you remember as being especially exciting, or funny, or frightening?

Research

Before you write your own story for young children, you need to know as much as possible about the kind of books they read. If possible you should look at a number of picture storybooks. Places to look:

At home
You may still have some of the books you had when you were younger – or there may be books belonging to younger brothers or sisters.

The local library
In the children's section you should be able to find a good selection of suitable books.

Questions to think about

What kind of central character?

For example:

animals
children
toys
adults
things (trains, cars etc)
fantasy creatures (goblins, witches etc)

What kind of story?

For example:

domestic (things that happen around the home)
adventure
mystery
finding out
hidden fears (for example going to the dentist)
fantasy

Just as one story can have different kinds of character, so it can also combine different story types from this list.

Talking to children

The best writing for young children comes from people who have first-hand experience of telling stories – often mothers who tell stories to their own children. This is how the well-known children's author Vivien Alcock remembers her start as a storyteller:

I said, 'What shall I tell you a story about ?' And Jane said, 'A toygum.' This was an imaginary animal and its different adventures – which, because of the need to think of a new story every night (and sometimes two new stories a night), was based roughly on her own life and experiences with a lot of dialogue to keep it going.

Unless you have a great deal of experience of young children, you may find it quite difficult to know how to set about writing a story for them. So it is a good idea to do some research:

At home
If you have younger brothers or sisters you can talk to them. Or talk to the young children in the families of relatives or friends.

At a local primary school
(If this can be arranged by your teacher.) The pictures on this spread were taken when the class from Avon did their local research.

What to do

1 Try to find out what sort of stories they enjoy.
2 Have a look at some of their books.
3 Talk to them about favourite characters.
4 Ask their parents or teachers about the stories which are most popular.
5 Try reading a story to them – or making one up and telling it to them.

Afterwards

Talk about, and then make some notes on, these points about the children and their stories:

1 Storylines in general.
2 Animals in stories – how do they behave?
3 Do objects like trains, tractors, aeroplanes, behave like human beings and talk and think and have feelings?
4 Do any of the stories deal with situations that the children might be expected to find worrying – for example going to hospital, starting school, a new baby in the family?
5 Did the children enjoy repetition?
6 Were opportunities for sound effects built into the stories (for example, hooting owls, choo-chooing trains)?
7 Did the children enjoy 'hands-on' books (for example, with flaps to lift or dials to spin)?

Planning

Before you can start writing, you need to think about your story and the way in which it will be told. Different people do their planning in different ways. Some like to start by deciding the kind of book they are going to produce. Others, like Berlie Doherty, begin with ideas for the story and then think about questions like who the story is for afterwards:

> *Very often I'm not sure what age group I'm actually going to be writing for when I start writing. I've got perhaps a character or a place or an image of some sort in my head. Then very often it'll start settling down, so the central character is a particular person who is a particular age. That then seems to be the focal age of the story.*

There are three questions you need to answer:

What kind of story?

The questions at the bottom of page 157 may help you to decide.

What kind of audience?

- How old are they?
- Will they be able to read the story themselves?
- Will the story be read to them while they look at the pictures?

What kind of book?

Think about the answers to these questions:

1 What is the balance between words and pictures?
2 How big should my book be – A4, or A5 (A4 folded in half), or some other size?
3 How many lines of writing on a page?
4 How many words to a line?
5 What kind of print or writing should the text be in?
6 Will there be any lift-up flaps, pop-ups or other devices?

Making and using pictures

You should remember that pictures are very important in books for young children. They often tell parts of the story that are not told in words.

1 Have a very clear idea in your head what the picture is meant to show: what part of the story it tells.
2 If you are not very confident about drawing, do simple outline drawings, like the Mr Men.
3 Another approach is to build up pictures using elements cut out from magazines and comics.

Look at the examples on this page and see how the students from Avon tackled the problem.

Appletree Farm was a very peaceful farm. All the animals were good friends.

FRIDDIP

Next Ben met a frog. 'Friddip, Friddip' said the frog as it swam through the water

'Can I swim like you?' Ben asked the frog. 'No, you can't swim' said the frog and went on his way.

FRIDDIP

Writing

Do ...

- remember that your readers are probably not yet very experienced. As a writer you need to give them all the help you can
- enjoy playing with words
- try to write with a rhythm
- use repetition if it helps to put the story across
- begin the story with an exciting, strange or funny sentence that will catch their attention.

Don't ...

- use words that are too long or difficult for your readers
- write sentences that are too long – they will get lost
- talk down to them.

Good advice

Geraldine Kaye, a professional writer, says that one of her secrets is:

As I'm writing, I read out loud all the time. Every page or so, I'll read it out loud, because I think the sound, the music of the line is very important.

Drafting

The only way to 'get it right' is to write and rewrite and rewrite yet again until you are *sure* that your sentences are as good as they can be.

The process

1 Drafting

Start with a rough draft of the writing. Work on this until you are satisfied with it before starting the final version.

As with other kinds of writing, it is a great help if you can work with someone else. Ask them to read what you have written and comment on it.

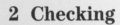

2 Checking

Your audience may not be very experienced readers, so it is very important to give them a text that is as accurate as you can make it.

3 Presentation

Before you start to write your final version, you must think about how you want to present it and also about some of the practicalities of making it into a book.

Think about:

1 Title
2 Cover design
3 Cover illustration

4 Performance: the final test!

Go back to the children you spoke to before… and read your story to them. (Or ask them to read it to you, if they can.)

Was it successful?

Practicalities

Single sheet/double sheet
Your book can be made in one of two ways:

- as single sheets pinned together
- as double sheets folded down the middle.

What goes where
If you are using double sheets folded, you need to think about what book page goes on each part of the sheets of paper you are using.

Binding
You have to fix the pages together using:

- treasury tags
- ring binder
- staples (and if you're using double sheets folded, that means you need a long-armed stapler).

Cover
Think about:

- what it will be made of
- how you will protect it (book-covering film and laminating are good methods, but not cheap).

Testing, testing

Page	Title	What you do	Why you do it
163	**Testing, testing**	Look at some puzzles, try to work out the answers, and then talk about them.	To introduce the themes of the unit.
164–165	**How fast are your reactions?**	With a partner, develop and try out a test of skill. Write a report on it.	To practise writing instructions and reports.
166–168	**Examination**	Read an extract from an autobiography and answer the questions on it, including writing about it in your own words. Think about proverbs.	To develop your skills as a reader and writer.
169	**A test of betting**	Read a newspaper extract and think about the issues it raises.	To distinguish between fact and opinion in a text. To practise expressing your own opinions and backing them up.
170-173	**Testing understanding**	Read two illustrated texts and make up a test that will show whether someone has understood one of them. Try out your test with a partner and then improve it. Use the information in the texts to write a paragraph about recycling.	To understand more clearly what is involved in testing understanding. To develop your ability to extract information from a text and use it in your own writing.
174–178	**Cheers, whistles, drama...it's a driving test**	Read an article, and show that you have understood it. Comment on the issues raised in the article and answer questions testing your detailed understanding of it.	To develop your close reading skills.

TESTING, TESTING

1 The three glasses on the left are full of liquid; the others are empty. Move just one glass so that the glasses stand alternately empty and full.

2 Assuming that people's left feet are of a similar shape to their right feet, how many different people have crossed the patch of sand on the right?

3 A plate with a question written on it has broken into six pieces (one of them is upside down). Put them together correctly and answer the question.

4 Which of the pieces with letters could not have come from the diagram at the bottom?

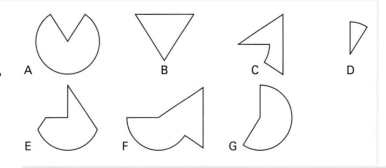

A   B   C   D
E   F   G

*Clive Doig's
Radio Times
Puzzle Book*

Can you do them?

- Can you work out the right answers to these puzzles?
- Can you prove that they are right?
- What skills do you think these puzzles test?

How fast are your reactions?

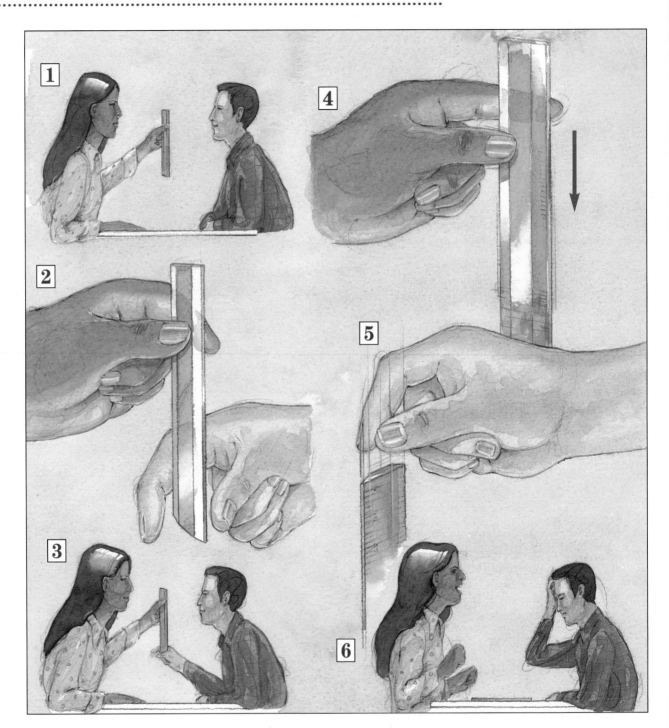

- Have you ever played this game?
- Are you any good at it?
- Who is best at it in your class?

Making a test

The game illustrated opposite tests the speed of a person's reactions. The simple test is whether you can catch the ruler at all. But even people who always catch the ruler can compete – you can measure their skill by looking at *where* they catch the ruler. You are going to devise a similar simple test and try it out on a partner.

1 Thinking

Begin by deciding what you are going to test. Here are some possibilities:

- how good someone is at distinguishing two colours that are similar
- how quickly a person can read and understand a passage of writing
- someone's sense of touch.

2 Planning

- Think carefully about *how* you will test the skill you have chosen.
- Make notes of what you decide.
- Sort your test into a **sequence** (the correct order in which you are going to do things).
- Collect together any equipment you will need.
- Make sure that you can explain carefully to the other person exactly what is to be done and why.

3 Testing

Work with a partner
Take it in turns to try out your tests on each other. Make notes on how the test went – and, if it went wrong, why it did.

4 Reporting

Now write a report on your test and how it went. Include these points:

- a description of the skill being tested
- a stage-by-stage description of the test you devised
- a description of what happened when you tried it out
- your ideas on how the test could be improved.

Examination

The classroom was very quiet. The twelve o'clock buzzer had gone, and all who were not taking the examination had gone to dinner. So had many of the candidates. Either because they had done as much as they could do, or like their fathers and mothers did not like the sense of being separated from their friends and fellows, most of the young examinees had handed in their papers and gone. Once outside the school they ran off into the streets like fish returned to the stream. Only a handful of boys was now left, and the only sounds in the room were the gurgling of the pipes, the scraping of hobnail boots on the iron crosspieces of the desks, and the scratching of pens. As the minutes ticked by, one more candidate gave in, and his rough boots clattered over the floor of the classroom as he went up to hand in his paper. In the end there was only one boy left. When he looked up and found he was alone he felt a momentary pang of alarm. He was too engrossed to be seriously troubled, but he must have looked a little anxious because the teacher stirred and spoke. It was Mr Cresswell, a teacher whom the boys generally feared. He was irritable and impatient and at times violent. Yet when he spoke it was in a kind voice. 'Don't hurry, Kirtley. The examination goes on until half past. You have plenty of time left.'

10

It was a pleasant surprise to hear him speak in so gentle a voice, and the boy was suddenly inspired with a tremendous resolution, almost with obstinacy. He would not be rushed. He hadn't finished yet, but there was nothing wrong in not having finished. The time was still his and he was determined to use it.

He worked quickly, looking up from time to time. In these little intervals he did not seem to observe anything, yet everything imprinted itself upon his brain – the old stained map on the wall, so dark and brown that hardly any detail could be seen on it, the queer grain, like contour lines, on the cheap yellow cupboards, the long cobwebs hanging from the high ceiling, and Mr Cresswell's bent right arm, the arm that had been damaged in the war. He looked down and returned to the last questions .

'Write down in your own words the meaning of the following proverbs: "A rolling stone gathers no moss." …'

It was difficult to find new words for that, but he wrestled with his vocabulary and found an equivalent. He struggled with all the proverbs and as the hand on the discoloured school clock moved towards the half-hour, he ruled off and gave in his paper. There was a moment of solitude as he stood, the only boy in the great empty playground, but he pulled on his cap, kicked a stone before him, and ran home.

As he drew near to home he could hear the familiar sounds of a collier washing-day – the thumping of the poss-sticks in the wash tubs, a rhythmic boom-boom as the wooden possers beat against the bottom of the tubs; and when he turned the corner he saw the lines of washing all strung out across the muddy streets. One of those poss-sticks being pounded up and down in the tub and one of those lines belonged to his mother.

When he got home he found her in a kitchen full of steam and the unpleasant odour of washing. The floor was covered with piles of dirty clothes, all sorted into whites and coloureds; and every flat space was occupied by her paraphernalia – scrubbing-brushes, tins of blue, bowls of starch, slabs of yellow soap, and pegs. Francis's mother was always in a disagreeable mood on washing-day; she was even more cross at his coming home at this inconvenient time.

'A nice day to pick for an examination, I must say,' she said. 'You would have thought they'd have enough sense to keep off a washing-day, at any rate. Well, you'll have to slip down to Mrs Cairns', and get yourself a pie and a few peas, because I canna be bothered with you.'

Frederick Grice: *The oak and the ash*

poss-stick, posser: a wooden tool used to hit the washing with, to force the soapy water through the material

Thinking points

1 When do you think this story takes place? What evidence suggests this to you?
2 What kind of school is described?
3 At the time of this story, the only common way of assessing how much students had learned was an examination of the kind described. Today examinations are still used, but students are also commonly assessed *continuously*, using marks for **coursework**, **projects**, or **short tests** done at intervals during the term. What are the advantages and disadvantages of these different kinds of assessment?

Proverbs

In the examination the boy had to explain the meaning of a proverb.

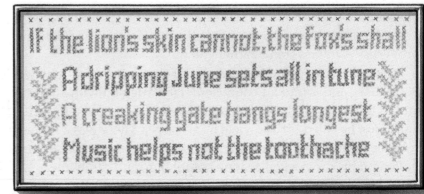

1 What are proverbs?
2 How many can you think of?
3 What use are they?
4 Choose four proverbs, write them out and explain what you think they mean.

Writing about the passage

1 The first paragraph is about the atmosphere in the classroom towards the end of the examination:

■ Describe this atmosphere using your own words.
■ Explain how the writer communicates it to you.

2 How does the teacher speak to the boy and how does he respond?
3 What impression do you get of the boy's home and of his mother?

> ### Writing advice
>
> For more advice about answering questions that test your understanding, look at pages 180–182.

A test of betting

How would you feel if your parents started staking money on your examination results? Strange as it may seem, more and more parents are doing just that. This is how the trend was reported in the *Daily Express*.

PARENTS BET ON EXAM CHILDREN

PARENTS ARE PICKING UP thousands of pounds gambling on their children's exam results. But last night teachers and psychologists condemned their money-making, and said it put children under too much pressure.

'It is horrifying,' said education expert Dr David Fontana. 'Look at the lesson you are teaching – not only that it is OK to gamble, but that you can treat a child as a substitute for a racehorse.'

And the head teacher John Sutton said the pupils' work could be seriously damaged by the extra stress.

'Parents should consider the effects of putting any further pressure to succeed on their children,' he added.

As the exam season gets under way bookmakers William Hill say they are taking more and more bets on GCSE and A-level results.

And so far the parents have had rich pickings.

'We have not had one loser, so we have had to shorten the odds on youngsters passing their exams,' said Hill's spokesman Graham Sharpe. 'Parents are using their winnings to reward their children with mountain bikes, clothes, or even a car.'

Hill's credit teenager Andrew Wright of Hummersknott School Darlington, with inventing the new form of gambling.

In 1990 Andrew, then 16, persuaded his doctor father to place a £50 wager on him gaining A grades in all his GCSE exams at 20–1 – and he won £1,000.

Last summer mathematics lecturer Mick Misra won nearly £500 after his daughter Sheila collected nine GCSE A grades. Fred Mycock, from Cleveleys, Lancashire, made £200 when his son Scott passed four A-levels with A grades.

And a Cardiff doctor will win £5,000 if his daughter chalks up nine GCSE A grades this year.

Daily Express

Fact and opinion

Most newspaper and magazine articles are a mixture of facts about what is happening and opinions about it. This is no exception.
Pick out what you think are the two most important facts and the two most important opinions in this report.

What do you think? TF

Dr Fontana and John Sutton both think that placing bets on exam results is wrong. What are their reasons? Do you agree with them? What are your reasons?

Testing understanding: texts TF

Read the texts on these two pages and then look at pages 172–173.

The problem of sewage

A city of one million people produces about 500,000 tonnes of sewage every year. In most developed countries this sewage is processed to make it safe before it is flushed into the sea or rivers. But even today a large amount is dumped into the sea partly treated or even untreated.

The problem is even greater in the developing countries because processing facilities are often poor, and much of the partly-treated sewage runs into rivers that are also used to provide water supplies, not just to the fields, but often to whole villages.

Household waste

Disposing of household waste is a major task for any city. Each day produces a mountain of paper, glass, tin cans, food scraps and other domestic waste.

Most domestic rubbish is buried, but suitable sites near cities are harder and harder to find. Also, people are now becoming more concerned about wasting the Earth's resources by burying rubbish that could be reused or recycled. The result is that waste is now sorted. Rubbish that cannot be reused is still buried, or burned in incinerators, but more and more of the glass, metal and paper is now recycled.

Recycling waste such as glass, paper and tin saves on the Earth's resources that are used to make these things. In addition, recycling saves on fuel since less heat is needed to recycle things than to make them from the beginning.

Glass bottles and jars are collected in bottle banks and then melted down to make new glass. Paper and card can be pulped and made into paper again. The tin and aluminium in metal cans is often melted down to make new cans, instead of mining more metal. Vegetable matter can be left in a compost heap where it will rot back into the earth.

Martyn Bramwell

Pure genius in the making of a can

It's ultra-thin and very strong, produced using the latest technology. But, best of all, it holds beer. **Steve Connor** reports

The modern beer can has reached the parts of technological perfection that the other consumer products cannot reach.

Today's lightweight beverage cans are made of aluminium that is as thin as two pages of this newpaper, yet when formed into the shape of a tube can support the weight of an average adult, this month's Scientific American says.

'Produced by the hundreds of millions every day, the modern can . . . is a tribute to precision design and engineering.'

More aluminium beverage cans are produced each year than nails or paperclips – 100 billion in the US alone – yet each can withstand a pressure three times greater than a car tyre, while using almost one-third less metal than 30 years ago.

Such lightweight strength is the result of the sort of precision and attention to the detail that goes into the design of an aircraft's wing, according to the metallurgists William Hosford, of the University of Michigan, and John Duncan, of Auckland University in New Zealand.

Professor Hosford and Professor Duncan describe how the evolution of the beverage can has reduced the amount of aluminium and the energy used in making each can. Can makers are aiming to reduce the weight of a can by a further 20 per cent, they say.

'Reducing the can's mass by one per cent will save approximately $20m (£13.3m) a year in aluminium.'

Despite using less aluminium, manufacturers have increased the strength of cans by dissolving magnesium into the material, which slightly distorts the molecular structure of the metal making it better able to resist deformations.

Flattening and rolling the aluminium sheets at room temperatures prior to making a can also increases the strength of the metal, enabling manufacturers to shave a few more thousandths of a millimetre off the wall of a container.

It takes energy equivalent to a 100W light bulb being lit for six hours to make one aluminium can, the researchers say.

'One way to reduce this expense is through recycling, which can save up to 95 per cent of the energy cost.'

Space technology and the beer can

Flange is bent and seamed to secure lid.

How the hinge works

Lid can be 25 % of total weight because of extra strength needed.

Rivet is integral piece of the lid to act as hinge for the tab.

Angled neck of can allows smaller lid to save on weight.

Aluminium alloy wall ironed to dimensions of within 0.0001 inch, made thicker at bottom for added integrity. It withstands internal pressure of 90 psi and can support 250 lbs.

Mirror-like finish from ironing process.

Dome-shaped base to resist internal pressure.

The Independent

Testing understanding

Different kinds of question

If you want to test whether someone has understood a text, there are several different kinds of question you can ask them. All the examples below are based on *The problem of sewage* on page 170. You can try them out by seeing if you can answer them yourself.

Straight questions
These can be:

- detailed factual questions that focus on a small part of the text:

  Is all sewage treated before it is pumped into the sea?

- questions that ask the reader to look at a larger part of the text and think about it:

  Why do developing countries have greater problems in sewage disposal than developed countries?

True/false questions
These offer a statement and ask whether it is true or false:

  A city of two million people produces 500,000 tonnes of sewage a year. True or false?

Multiple choice
These ask a question and then offer a choice of answers, one of which is correct:

  Why do developing countries have greater problems in sewage disposal than developed countries?

  A because they don't process the drinking water
  B because they drink the water straight out of the river
  C because sewage flows into the rivers they use for drinking water without being properly treated
  D because they don't know any better.

Wider activities
You can also test understanding by setting up a writing task or other activity. The person being tested can only complete the activity properly if they have understood the text.

  Make a list of things that can be done to improve sewage disposal by:

  - *developed countries*
  - *developing countries.*

1 Make your own test

Now it's your turn. You are going to make up a test to check whether someone has understood one of the passages on pages 170–171.

1 Choose **either** *Household waste* **or** *Pure genius in the making of a can*.
   Note: the second is longer and harder than the first!
2 Read the passage carefully two or three times to make sure that you have fully understood it.
3 Make a list of the facts you want to set questions on. Try to get a mix of detailed sections and a broader approach to large parts of the text.
4 For each one decide what kind of question you will set.
5 Write out a rough list of questions.
6 Go through them carefully, making sure that each one is clear: will another person understand *exactly* what they are being asked?

2 Trialling

Work with a partner

1 Swap tests.
2 Do your partner's test. (Write out the answers as carefully as if it were a test your teacher had set!)
3 Swap back and mark the test you set.
4 Return them and discuss what you thought of each other's test and how it might be improved.
5 **On your own**, write a revised version of your test.

3 Recycling the texts

EXT

1 The texts on both pages make reference to **recycling**. Read them again, picking out the sections where it is mentioned.
2 Make notes on all the facts and opinions about recycling contained in both texts.
3 Write a paragraph explaining:

   ■ what recycling is and why, in general, it is important
   ■ which materials are commonly recycled
   ■ how the manufacture of drinks cans is a good example of the need to economise on raw materials and recycle waste.

Cheers, whistles, drama ...

... it's a driving test

Along with 80 other sacrificial lambs taking their
driving tests, I arrived at the police stadium in Qatar at
5am. We were commanded to form a queue in alphabetical
order, which took us until six o'clock. Then the fun started.

The first event on the agenda was the eye test, and I was directed to
the medical room, which had a deceptively high step at its entrance. I
entered the room by sprawling headlong on to the floor. The medical
officer, sitting behind an impressive oak desk and with a baton under his
arm, peered down at me over his glasses.

10   'I've come to take the eye test,' I said.

'Really?' he said. 'Not a very good start, is it?'

Half an hour later, it was on to the police interview room for the oral
test to identify road signs, a seemingly pointless exercise, as if there's one
thing that's completely ignored in Qatar, it's the road signs. I was directed
to an officer who was sitting at a desk on which were stacked about 20
worn cards, each depicting a different sign.

He held up a card. 'You know this?'

It was upside down. 'Yes,' I said.

He stared back at me suspiciously, returned the card to the pile and
20   then held up a second.

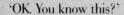'OK. You know this?'

I looked intently at the card, and once again replied: 'Yes.' He had a third go. 'OK,' he said, holding the card he'd started with – still upside down. 'You know this?'

'Yes,' I said quickly, not wishing to change a winning formula. The officer thought for a moment, then said: 'OK, pass, go.'

On to the obstacle course. For the next three hours I was to witness a scene of carnage performed to the din of crashing obstacles, jeering spectators – other candidates and their families who had come along for the fun – and policemen's whistles. Two identical courses had been constructed, each comprising three different obstacles, so six drivers were under test simultaneously.

A policeman was allocated to each obstacle. He would signify if you'd failed by blowing his whistle, signify if you'd passed by blowing his whistle, and signify all other instructions, as well as his tea break, by blowing his whistle.

It was now almost 10 o'clock and the temperature in the shade was 122°F. I was second in the line of vehicles waiting to enter the stadium, behind a young Filipino who looked terrified. He was meant to have parked with his front wheels just behind a white line at the stadium entrance, but had stopped too far forward. When a policemen noticed this, he immediately blew his whistle at the poor guy and waved at him to pull back.

This he did, reversing straight into me. Unfortunately, although in neutral, I had forgotten to apply my handbrake, and immediately ricocheted into the car behind which did have its handbrake on, causing me to rebound and whack the rear of the Filipino. We had managed a triple collision before we'd even started.

The first obstacle required the driver to reverse through two rows of metal posts, placed in an S shape, with the gap between each row looking marginally less than the width of the car. The posts fell at the slightest contact, resulting in failure.

The Filipino drove slowly towards the two rows of posts on his way to the starting point, and hit the first post he reached. The policeman in charge of the obstacle blew his whistle. The crowd of about 200 cheered. The poor guy's driving test had lasted 10 seconds.

It was now my turn. I drove slowly into the S obstacle and through to the starting point. As I began reversing, there was an almighty crash from across the stadium. Two other cars had collided head-on.

The policeman in charge of the S immediately dashed across to assist. I took the opportunity to reverse, at a considerably slower speed than is allowed, through the full length of the obstacle and the man returned as I emerged unscathed at the finish. He looked surprised. 'OK, go,' he said, blowing his whistle and pointing to my next destination.

The Heinemann English Programme 3

This was the L obstacle, a steep ramp about the height of a double-decker bus. The object was to reverse halfway up between the posts, stop, drive back down, then reverse up again, this time to the top, then negotiate a right-angle bend before the ramp levels off – at which point you stop. As I reached the start, another driver was about to begin his ascent. He was
70 already in the reverse position. I could clearly see the fear in his eyes.

He completed the first part surprisingly efficiently, but at the top his luck ran out. As he manoeuvred around the right angle bend, he gently touched one of the posts which fell with a clank. The policeman blew his whistle. He'd failed.

Unfortunately, his disappointment must have caused him to panic. Instead of applying the footbrake, he obviously hit the accelerator and shot backwards before shuddering to a halt with his rear wheels hanging in mid-air over the side of the ramp. There was a moment of total silence, then all hell broke loose.

80 From all directions, whistle-blowing policemen appeared. Five of them clung grimly to the front of the car to stop it plunging groundwards, not helped by the driver, who naturally preferred to get out, ignoring the fact that it was only his weight that was anchoring it to the ramp. The last I saw of him, he was being escorted away by practically the entire Qatari police force.

Next it was my turn, but I was lucky. No sooner had I reversed halfway up the ramp than the policeman, presumably confused by events, blew his whistle, waved me away and said, 'OK, go,' and indicated that I should proceed to the last obstacle – the P.

90 This final hurdle was a parking bay, made up of collapsible posts, into which the car had to be reversed – a formidable task, as the bay appeared to be of a size sufficient only to accommodate a bicycle.

I drove slowly backwards, and was halfway into the bay when I just touched two of the posts and watched in my wing mirror as they simultaneously began to fall.

Then the posts, presumably placed too closely together, struck each other on their way down and miraculously balanced against each other, like the tip of an arrow. For a few seconds they shuddered. The policeman hesitated, willing them to fall. The crowd laughed and began throwing
100 rubbish to knock them over ... but they didn't fall. The policeman slowly withdrew the whistle from his lips, disappointment clouding his features.

So I'd passed the driving test. I constituted 50 per cent of the successful candidates that morning; the other 50 per cent was an off-duty policeman.

The Independent

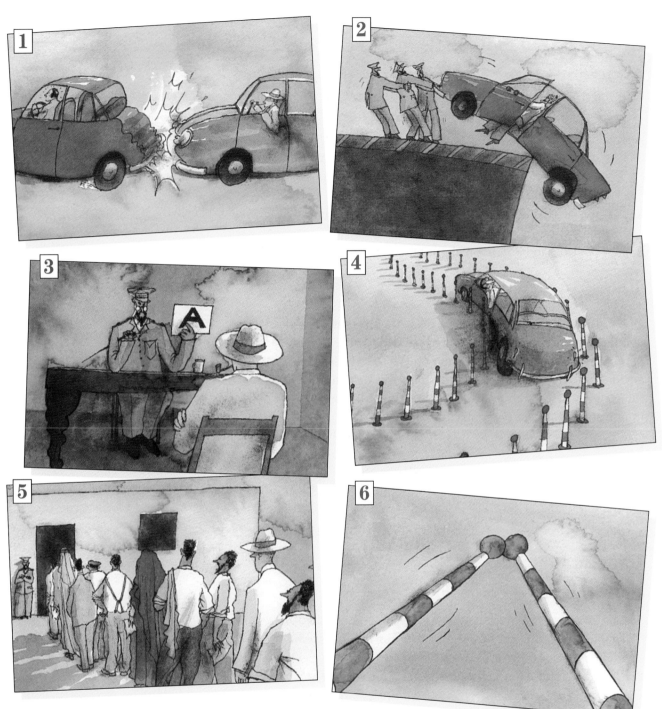

Sort it out

These six pictures illustrate the article you have just read – but they are in the wrong order.

1 Work out the correct order.
2 Write the numbers of the pictures in the order they should be.
3 Think of a suitable caption for each picture and write it alongside the number for that picture.

It's funny, but is it fair?

You probably found parts of the article on pages 174–176 amusing – the writer certainly meant you to.

1 Which parts did you find amusing?
2 Exactly what were you laughing at?
3 The writer is a European and at the time was presumably working in Qatar, an Arab country. How would you feel about the article if you were a Qatari?
4 Is it possible to argue that the article is just poking fun at foreigners?
5 Is it possible to be funny without hurting someone's feelings?

Accident prone

One of the entertaining aspects of the article is that several people (including the author) were 'accident-prone'. Some people seem to be more likely than others to have small accidents – tripping up, knocking things over, saying the wrong thing. Write a story about a person like this. Choose an important day in that person's life. For example:

- a birthday
- the day of an important exam
- when they are picked for a school sports team (but you'll have to think about *why* they would be picked)
- a case of mistaken identity.

Understanding

Answer these questions on the article you have just read.

1 The writer clearly does not have a very high opinion of the way in which the test was conducted. How is this shown in his description of the test of identifying road signs?
2 Choose one of the practical tests and explain clearly:

- what candidates had to do
- what the difficulties were
- what driving skills were being tested.

3 What driving skills were the other practical parts of the examination designed to test?
4 What were the main reasons why the practical part of the examination was so chaotic?

Writing advice

For more advice about answering questions that test your understanding, look at pages 180–182.

Tackling reading

There are good and bad ways of approaching reading a text, especially if you are going to be tested on how well you have understood it. On this page and the next, we suggest one way of tackling reading for a test.

1 Skimming

Start by reading the text quickly ('skimming') to get the gist of what it is about.

2 Questioning

Jot down any questions that come into your mind.

3 Reading it again carefully

This time take it more slowly and try to understand as much as possible of the text.

4 Marking up

- Divide the text up into the main sections.
- You may find it helps to give each one a title.
- Underline any parts that you think are very important.
- Mark any parts that you find particularly difficult.

5 Reading the questions

- Read them all.
- Go through them one at a time and make sure that you really understand them.
- Go through them again and find the sections of the text that they refer to.
- Look at the box headed 'Answering the questions' on page 180.

6 Making notes

Go through the questions again and make notes on each one.

7 Writing your answers

Look at the box headed 'Writing an answer' on page 180.

Answering the questions

The questions in end-of-year tests are often quite 'big'. They ask you to think about quite a large section of the text. This means that everyone has a chance to get some marks, but it also means that it is easy to miss out something important.

SO:

1 Read the question very carefully.
2 Make sure you understand it fully.
3 Look carefully at any prompts it gives you.
4 Think about the different parts it can be divided into.
5 Find the section(s) of the text that contain the information you need.
6 Use it to find the answer.
7 Make notes.
8 Check question and text again to make sure that you have got the whole answer.

Writing an answer

If you are answering a 'big' question, you will almost certainly need to write several sentences.

SO:

1 Make notes before you write.
2 Be sure that you have evidence to back up everything you say.
3 Write most of the answer **using your own words**.
4 Use some **direct quotations** to support your answer, but use quotation marks.
5 Get your material into a sensible order before you start writing.
6 When you have finished, check your work to make sure that it is:

   ■ complete
   ■ correct
   ■ accurate.

Tackling writing

There is no one way to approach a piece of writing. Some tasks will require much more thought, planning and checking than others. But every piece of writing goes through the same main stages. If you keep these in mind when you start work, it will help you to write clearly and effectively.

1 Thinking

Whatever you write you need to do some thinking before you start. Sometimes you can do it all in your head and on your own; at other times you may need to write things down and work with other people. Here are some of the things you need to cover:

Defining the subject
Make sure you understand *exactly* what you are being asked to write about. A good way of doing this is to describe what it means in your own words.

Generating ideas
You can do this on your own or in a group, in your head or on paper:

- Group brainstorming
  - appoint someone to write ideas down
  - give yourselves a short period of time – say two or three minutes
  - everyone says any idea that comes into their heads about the subject
  - all ideas are written down
  - no one criticises or makes fun of what is said.

- Web diagram
  - use a large piece of paper and put the subject in a circle in the centre
  draw lines out to the main ideas you have about it
  - do the same with each of these ideas
  - and so on …

2 Planning

There are two main aspects to this:

Research
You may need to collect information from:

- your own books
- the library
- people you ask
- material you write away for.

Sorting
You certainly need to work out the order in which you want to present your material. If it is a short piece of writing, you may be able to do this in your head. Often you will need to write some notes.

3 Drafting

There are many different ways of expressing an idea. Drafting is the process of working out what is the best way of saying what you want to say. It can be done in many different ways:

- In your head. You work out exactly what you are going to say before you start writing. This can work well for very short pieces. Otherwise you have to be some kind of genius for it to work at all.
- Writing a rough version, changing it, and then writing a second (and even a third version) until you are satisfied with what you have written.
- Using a word processor. (Much the same as using paper, except that usually you lose the old version and so cannot look back at it.)

It is often a good idea to get someone else – teacher, parent, friend – to read what you have written and make suggestions about it. If that is impossible, then try leaving it for as long as possible before you read it through.

4 Polishing

Once you have got the text into the shape you want, you have to 'polish' it up so that it is easy and enjoyable to read and understand.

- Check your work for errors of:
  - grammar
  - spelling
  - punctuation.
- Write out the final version in your best handwriting, with good margins.

Grammar

Grammar describes how language works:

- how words are arranged to make sentences
- the ways in which some words are changed to fit into sentences.

It is useful to know how sentences work. It can help you to:

- overcome problems you meet when reading and writing
- talk to other people (eg your teacher) about your writing.

Sentences

There are four different kinds of sentence. Each one is used for a different purpose. Each follows a different pattern.

Statement *I like music.*

Question There are three types:
Yes/no questions *Do you like music?*
Wh- questions *What kind of music do you like?*
Either/or questions *Do you like rock or classical?*

Directive *Play that music!*
Directives have many different purposes (for example to command, request, warn, advise).

Exclamation *What a great song that is!*

Parts of a sentence

Every full statement sentence contains a subject and a verb. Many sentences contain other parts after the verb. The parts of a sentence may be a single word, or a group of words, a *phrase*.

Subject
The subject of a statement sentence comes at the beginning of the sentence and often tells us what the sentence will be about:

My friend Alison Greenaway *won the race.*

Verb

In a statement sentence the verb comes after the subject:

> *My friend Alison Greenaway **won** the race.*

The subject of the sentence can be singular or plural. The verb must agree with the subject:

> *Alison **likes** athletics. / My sister and I **like** netball.*

When we are writing or speaking, the events we describe can take place in the past, the present or the future. We can show this in two ways:

- by using time words like *yesterday, next week*
- by the **tense** of the verb:

Present tense	**Past tense**
I walk	I walked
she walks	she walked

Tenses can take different forms:

> *As I **was walking** to school I **met** Dave.*

This is called the past **continuous**. We use it for actions that go on (continue) for a period of time.

This is the **simple** past. We use it mainly for simple completed actions.

The verb in a sentence may consist of one word, or a group of words, a **verb phrase**. A verb phrase always contains a **full** verb, like *see*. The easiest way to think of full verbs is that nearly all of them have meanings that you can explain to somebody. For example if a foreigner asked you the meaning of *see*, you could explain, or show them what it means. So *see* is a full verb.

The verb phrase may also contain one or more **auxiliary** verbs. These do not have a meaning that you can explain or show, but they help the full verb to express its meaning:

Full verbs	*Auxiliary verbs*
chase	may
munch	will

> **Warning**
> There are two verbs that can be full verbs *or* auxiliary verbs:
> *be/is/am* etc
> *have/had* etc

Object

As well as a subject and a verb, many sentences contain an object. This comes after the verb in a statement sentence and it refers to a different person or thing from the subject:

> *Alison likes **athletics**.*

Complement

In some sentences, the verb may be followed by a complement. As its name suggests, a complement completes the meaning of another part of the sentence:

SUBJECT   VERB   COMPLEMENT
My name   *is*   *Mary*

Sentences like this contain a special kind of verb sometimes called a linking verb: *is, seem, appear, become.*

There is more about this on page 66.

Adverbial

Some sentences have a section after the verb that is neither an object nor a complement:

SUBJECT   VERB   ADVERBIAL
Some lessons *seem to last* *forever*

An adverbial can be one word or a group of words. It answers questions like When?, Where?, How?, How much?, Why?

Phrases

A phrase is a group of words forming part of a sentence. A phrase does not contain a complete verb. There are three main types of phrase:

Verb phrases
The verb in a sentence can be one word or a number of words. If the verb is made up of more than one word it is called a verb phrase.

Noun phrases
These always have a noun as the main word:

*a **teacher***
*an interesting **teacher***
*an unusual, clever and interesting **teacher***
*an unusual, clever and interesting **teacher** with a fast sports car*

Noun phrases can be the **subject**, **object** *or* **complement** in a sentence.

Prepositional phrases
These always begin with a preposition. The commonest use of prepositional phrases is as the **adverbial** in a sentence:

*I left my books **on the bus**.*

Words

The words we use to build sentences can be grouped into different classes according to the way in which they are used. It is useful to know the names of these classes so that you can use them when you are talking about your own writing and other people's.

Noun

Nouns are words that refer to people, places, things and ideas. They answer the questions 'What?' or 'Who?'

Nouns can be formed from verbs, adjectives, and other nouns, by adding a suffix, like *-er, -ness, -ment, -ity.*

Pronoun

Pronouns stand in place of nouns, or groups of words doing the same work as nouns. We use them to avoid having to repeat the same noun over and over again. The **personal pronouns** are:

I	*me*
you	*you*
he/she/it	*him/her/it*
they	*them*

There are also **possessive pronouns:**

*He has a lot of CDs. That's one of **his** CDs.*

There are two types of possessive pronoun:

pronouns that always go with a noun	**pronouns that always stand alone**
*That's **her** book*	*That book is **hers**.*

There is more about this on page 86.

Adjective

Adjectives are words that help to make nouns more precise. They answer the question 'What kind of?'

Adjectives are used in two main ways:

- with a noun: '*My **red** car...*'
- after verbs like 'is': *My car is **red**.'*

Adjectives can be used to compare two or more things:

*Angela is **taller** than Jamie.*
*Peter is the **tallest** person in our class.*

We can also alter the meaning of an adjective by putting words before it:

*Peter is **very** tall.*

Verb

As we have seen, every full statement sentence contains a verb. The verb in a sentence can be one word or a number of words (called a **verb phrase**). If the verb in a sentence is made up of several words, these are all called verbs. Confusing, but that's the way it is.

Adverb

Adverbs work with verbs and answer questions like 'How?' 'When?' and 'Where?'

> He left **quickly**.   He jumped **back**.   They returned **later**.

They are also used with adjectives and other adverbs (and then they answer the question 'How much?').

> He left **very** quickly.

Adverbs can be formed from adjectives, by adding the suffix -*ly*: *quickly*. Certain adverbs, like *really*, are used frequently in speech, without a lot of meaning.

There is more about this on page 106.

Preposition

Prepositions come before nouns or noun phrases:

> **on** the bus   **in** Manchester

There is more about prepositions on pages 40 and 41.

Parts of a word

Words can be built up from different parts.

Stem

Every word has a stem and many words consist of this alone: *happy, fortune*.

Prefix

A section that is added *before* the stem is called a prefix. Prefixes are used to change the meaning of a stem: **un**happy.

Suffix

A section that is added after the stem is called a suffix. Suffixes are used to change the class of a word. For example a noun can be changed into an adjective: *fortun**ate***.

Punctuation

We use punctuation marks to make our writing clear and easy to read. If you punctuate badly – or not at all – people will find it very difficult to understand your writing.

You will find information about capital letters and full stops in *The Heinemann English Programme* Books 1 and 2.

Comma

A comma is used to mark a pause or short break in a sentence. One common use for it is to separate things in a list.

Commas are also used to put things 'in brackets':

Mr Carter's boss, **John Thompson**, *thought the car was legally parked.*

Colon

Colons are used:
- to introduce a list
- before a piece of speech, instead of a comma

The key things to remember are:
- *go back to the shop*
- *take your receipt.*

Semi-colon

This marks a stronger pause or break than a comma. It is also sometimes used to separate things in a list.

It was a great bargain; I've not seen it cheaper elsewhere.

Apostrophe

There are two uses for the apostrophe:

- To show when one or more letters have been missed out:

  I have not → I haven't

- To show that something belongs to someone:

  The book belonging to Mary → Mary's book
  The car belonging to my parents → my parents' car

Setting out a script

There are a number of different ways of doing this. This is one which you can use, or adapt:

Setting
At the beginning of the scene you should describe where it takes place. Underline it and put it in brackets. This makes it clear that it is not words for an actor to speak.

Main stage directions
Actions that are done by more than one character, or actions by a character who is not speaking. They are kept separate from the spoken words. (In brackets and underlined.)

Character stage directions
These tell us what the character speaking is doing, or how s/he speaks the line. (In brackets and underlined.)

(The den – a hiding place that PAT and LIN and TERRY have built for themselves.)

(PAT, LIN, and TERRY rush in and throw themselves down. All are out of breath.)

PAT: (Still puffing) We're done for now.
LIN: (Looking out anxiously) Did anyone follow us?
PAT: No. (Pointing) Look, they're all still down by the swings.
TERRY: What if they find us?
PAT: They won't, we've spent weeks camouflaging this place.
LIN: (Worried) Are you sure?
PAT: Relax, we're safe here. Trust me.
TERRY: Yeah, you're right.

Words spoken
These are written normally, but with **no** inverted commas.

Character names
It helps if you always put these in capital letters – they are easier to see.
The names of speakers are put on the left hand side and followed by a colon (:).

Punctuating direct speech

Follow these rules for punctuating direct speech.

She hurried away from her tram-stop, rounded her street, saw a triangle of light thrown across the cobbles, and knew he was on the doorstep.

'What time d'you call this, you little hussy?' His voice echoed round the houses.

'Half past nine, Dad.' She knew it was no use lying. Lying was just as much a sin as disobedience was.

'Get in that house and up them stairs to your bed!'

She dodged under his arm and ran across the room where her brother Will was preparing his bath in front of the fire, and her mother sat darning at the table.

'Up them stairs!' roared her father as Bridie stopped

■ Each piece of speech begins and ends with inverted commas:
single : ❛ ❜
or double: ❝ ❞

■ Every **new** piece of speech starts with a capital letter, even if it is not the first word in the sentence.

■ When there is a new speaker, start a new line and indent.

■ If a piece of speech comes in the middle of a sentence it must have a comma, or a colon before the opening inverted comma(s).

■ Every piece of speech ends with a punctuation mark **before** the closing inverted comma(s). If it is the end of a sentence, use a full stop, question mark, or exclamation mark. If the sentence is going on, use a comma, a question mark or an exclamation mark.

Spelling

There is no simple way to become a good speller. Some people seem to find it easier than others. You can do something about it, however:

- Keep a spelling list (in the back of your English book, or in a separate notebook). Make sure that you write down the correct spelling of words you find difficult. Keep it in alphabetical order, or you will never be able to find the word you want.
- If there is a word you repeatedly get wrong, do this:

Look	at the word correctly spelled.
Cover	it up.
Write	it on a piece of paper.
Check	that you have got it right.

- If you are not sure which of two spellings is right, try writing them both out to see which one looks right.
- Use a dictionary to check your spelling.
- Above all, **read** as much as possible.

Common rules

Making plurals with 's'
- Usually, just add **s** .... books, ices
- Words that end in **s, x, ch, sh**, add **es** .... masses, taxes, branches, rushes
- Words that end in **y**
  if the letter before the **y** is a vowel, add **s** .... days
  if the letter before the **y** is a consonant,
  cut off the **y** and add **ies** .... babies
- Words that end in **f** or **fe**,
  change the **f/fe** to **ves** .... wolves
  Exceptions .... roofs, dwarfs, beliefs, chiefs, proofs
- Words that end in **o**, usually just add **s** .... pianos
  Exceptions .... tomatoes, potatoes, volcanoes, heroes

Adding -ing and -ed
Usually, you just add **ing** or **ed**, but there are some important special rules.
- words ending in **consonant + y**: .... try
  change the **y** to **i** before adding **ed** .... tried
- words of one syllable, with a
  long vowel ending in **e**: .... fade
  remove the **e** and add the ending .... faded fading
- words of one syllable, with a short
  vowel and ending in a single consonant: .... fit
  double the consonant and add the ending .... fitted fitting

-ie- or -ei-?

For words in which these letters make a long **ee** sound use:

i before **e** .... thief

except after **c** .... receive

Exceptions .... seize weir weird

-able/-ible

These two suffixes can cause people problems with spelling. The problem is that there is no clear rule. But the following advice may help:

1 All new words that are formed are spelled **-able**.
   skateboard → skateboardable

2 The list of words ending in **-ible** is quite short and some of them are not very well known.

3 Usually if you can remove the suffix and are still left with a proper word, then the suffix should be **-able**.
   affordable → afford

4 If you take the suffix away and what is left is not a proper word, then the suffix should be **-ible**.
   possible → poss

5 If the letter before the suffix is a hard 'c' or 'g', then the suffix is **-able**.
   practicable

6 These are the commonest words ending in **-ible**:

accessible	admissible	audible	collapsible	credible
edible	flexible	horrible	incredible	invisible
legible	possible	responsible	sensible	visible

-ant/-ent, -ance/-ence

- Words ending in **-ant/-ent** are usually adjectives.
- If a word can be spelled either way, the **-ant** version is a noun and the **-ent** version is an adjective: *independant* (n) *independent* (adj).
- If the adjective is spelled **-ant**, then the noun is spelled **-ance**: *important/importance* (and the same for **-ent/-ence**).
- If the suffix is preceded by a **t** or a **v**, then it is usually **-ant/-ance**.

Words that commonly cause problems

accelerate	accommodation	address	adviser
beginning	brilliant	caterpillar	collapse
collect	conscience	conscious	corridor
disappear	discuss	embarrass	encyclopaedia
exaggerate	forty	gaol	gauge
happiness	harass	imitate	immediate
millionaire	occasion	parallel	pedal
possess	professional	sheriff	success
terrible			